DS
558.2
.B45
1975

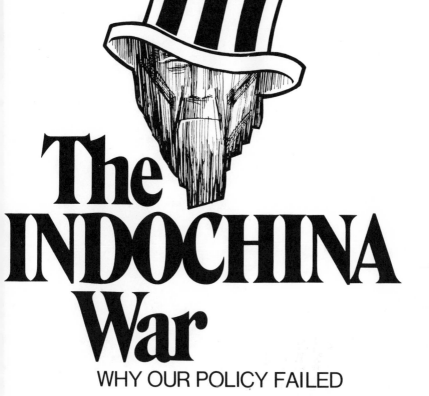

The
INDOCHINA
War
WHY OUR POLICY FAILED

OPPOSING VIEW  ven

DAVID L. BENDE
GARY E. McCUE
Editors

GREENHAVEN PRESS — ANOKA, MINNESOTA 55303

HIEBERT LIBRARY
Fresno Pacific College - M. B. Seminary 59905
Fresno, Calif. 93702

No part of this book may be reproduced or used in any form or by any means, electrical, mechanical or otherwise, including, but not limited to photocopy, recording or any information storage and retrieval system, without prior written permission from the publisher.

© Copyright 1975 by Greenhaven Press

ISBN 0-912616-18-0 Paper Edition
ISBN 0-912616-36-9 Cloth Edition

TABLE OF CONTENTS

TABLE OF EXERCISES

A major emphasis of this book is on critical thinking skills. Discussion exercises included after readings are not laborious writing assignments. They are included to stimulate class discussion and individual critical thinking.

INTRODUCTION

The Indochina War was one of the most controversial and frustrating episodes in American history. American involvement began under the Truman Administration in 1950 with economic and military aid to the French forces fighting in Indochina. It lasted until our withdrawal in April of 1975. As a result of the war, 56 thousand Americans were killed, 300 thousand were wounded and over 150 billion dollars were expended.

This volume presents students with a debate on the broad issues related to American participation in the Indochina War. Chapter one takes students back into the war years and examines arguments for and against continued U.S. participation in the conflict. A debate over why our policy failed is presented in chapter two and arguments about the lessons and consequences of the war are contained in chapter three. This volume examines American behavior in Indochina and raises basic questions about the goals and objectives of our foreign policy.

The **Opposing Viewpoints** format and **Discussion Activities** are vital aspects of this book. These features help teachers and students explore the kind of mindset, skills and attitudes that are necessary for intelligent analysis of magazines, newspapers, books, and all

1

kinds of printed matter. This format also should help raise some of the following questions:

1. How many people are aware that three of the most popular weekly news magazines, **Time**, **Newsweek** and **U.S. News & World Report** have a political slant and are not objective accounts of the news?

2. How many readers know there is no such thing as an objective author, book, newspaper or magazine?

3. How many people think that because a magazine or newspaper article is unsigned it is a statement of facts rather than opinions?

4. How can one determine the political slant of newspapers and magazines?

5. How does the editorial page of a newspaper differ from the other pages?

6. How many readers question an author's **frame of reference** (his training, political persuasion, and life experiences) when they read a book?

No doubt many people finish their formal education unable to cope with most of these basic questions. At best they will have little chance to understand the social forces and issues surrounding them. At worst one might say they have not received an education in any meaningful sense of that term. And some may fall victim to demagogues that preach solutions to problems by scapegoating minorities with conspiratorial and paranoid explanations of complex social issues.

The editors do not wish to imply that anything is inherently wrong with authors and publications that have a political slant or bias. All authors have a frame of reference because they are human, and readers should understand this reality. The **discussion exercises** after readings deal with separating *fact from opinion*, *bias from reason*, *primary from secondary sources*, *how to empathize*, and *how to recognize stereotyping, scapegoating, and ethnocentrism*. These discussion exercises along with the **Opposing Viewpoints** format hopefully will introduce students to the kind of questions they must ask and the skills they must learn to rationally analyze and interpret what they read.

2

CHAPTER 1

THE WAR YEARS

WAR CRITICS AID COMMUNISTS

Russell Long

Russell Long is a Democratic Senator from Louisiana. He was a leading Congressional spokesman supporting our military intervention in Vietnam during the Johnson Presidency.

Consider the following questions while reading:

1. Why did Senator Long believe the U.S. should continue its military activity in Vietnam?
2. Can you find any statements by Senator Long that are supported by the cartoon in this reading?
3. According to Senator Long, what made this country great? Do you agree?

Senator Russell Long, **Congressional Record**, February 16, 1966.

Mr. President, with my responsibilities of being chairman of a committee as well as the assistant majority leader, I was not able to be present at the hearings of the Foreign Relations Committee, but I want to say that these advocates of retreat, defeat, surrender, and national dishonor have not been doing the country any good when they went before a television network suggesting that this Nation was not committed to fighting aggression in this area. The Senate voted for the resolution last year, and Senators voted that this country would help that country resist aggression, and specifically authorized the President to take whatever steps he felt necessary to resist further aggression. We are committed. We have more than 200,000 men there. We have at stake our national honor. We are committed to resisting Communist aggression. That is what this is all about. It has been going on for some time.

RESISTING COMMUNIST AGGRESSION

First, and most important, is the simple fact that South Viet Nam, a member of the free-world family, is striving to preserve its independence from Communist attack. The Vietnamese have asked our help. We have given it. We shall continue to give it.

We do so in their interest; and we do so in our own clear self-interest. For basic to the principles of freedom and self-determination which have sustained our country for almost two centuries is the right of peoples everywhere to live and develop in peace. Our own security is strengthened by the determination of others to remain free, and by our commitment to assist them. We will not let this member of our family down, regardless of its distance from our shores.

Robert S. McNamara from a speech delivered before the National Security Industrial Association, Washington, D.C., March 26, 1964.

The Senator from Alaska voted against the resolution, and he was privileged to do it, but once the Congress adopted that resolution, it had taken a firm position. Once Congress authorized the President to do that which he felt necessary, the President was authorized to do it. It was authorized in the resolution and discussed specifically during the debate on the floor of the Senate. He was authorized to send troops wherever necessary to resist aggression in the area.

PEACE WITH HONOR

McElhattan in **The American Voice**, March, 1973

It is not helping our country when Senators go before the Nation and express their fears on this issue that the Red Chinese might come in, and the fact that we are losing some American boys. We are inflicting at least 10 to 1 damage on the North Viet-Nam invaders compared to the losses suffered by our forces.

If this great nation is to be humiliated, is to be defeated and run out and be downgraded to a second-class power by that little nation, then I wish Red China would come in. It would be a great humiliation for this Nation to be defeated by a small nation of 16 million people. If we must be defeated, it would be better to lose to a large nation of 700 million people.

This Nation was founded because we had courageous men. We became a great nation because the people had courage. They did not give up because they had to fight Indians. If the men who came on the *Mayflower* were frightened to helplessness the first time they had to fight Indians, they would have gone back to England on the *Mayflower*. But they fought the Indians and won, meanwhile losing some fine Americans, until this Nation became great. We are upholding our commitments in the proud tradition of our fathers, grandfathers, great-grandfathers, and many other courageous Americans who fell on the field of battle.

I only wish that back during the Civil War there had been a humorous element in the Congress that would have appeared daily before a nationwide television network and have said, "We fought and lost a Yankee today. We lost a boy today, let us quit." If they had spread that propaganda, it might have spread fear. Maybe the war would have gone the other way. Then we would have won the principles of States' rights. We would prove that we were the strong people. Having achieved victory we could have offered to rejoin the Union with considerable pride that our theory of States' rights had been sustained.

AMERICAN INTERVENTION PROMOTES COMMUNISM

J. William Fulbright

J. William Fulbright was a leading Senate war critic during the Johnson and Nixon administrations while serving as chairman of the Senate Foreign Relations committee. He was one of the nation's first elected public officials to question and criticize American military involvement in the Indochina War.

As you read try to answer the following questions:

1. According to Senator Fulbright, why should Americans not be too concerned over who rules the nations of Indochina?
2. What does he say about the Thieu Government in South Vietnam?
3. How does the cartoon in this reading support what Senator Fulbright is saying?

J. William Fulbright in a Senate speech on April 2, 1970.

8

It simply does not matter very much for the US, in cold, unadorned strategic terms, who rules the states of Indochina. Nor does it matter all that terribly to the inhabitants. At the risk of being accused of every sin from racism to Communism, I stress the irrelevance of ideology to poor and backward populations. Someday, perhaps, it will matter, in what one hopes will be a constructive and utilitarian way. But in the meantime, what earthly difference does it make to nomadic tribes or uneducated subsistence farmers, in Vietnam or Laos or the north of Thailand, whether they have a military dictator, a royal prince, or a socialist commissar in some distant capitol that they have never seen and may never even have heard of?

At their current stage of undevelopment these populations have more basic requirements. They need governments which will provide medical service and education, fertilizer, high-yield seeds and instruction in how to use them. They need governments which are honest enough to refrain from robbing and exploiting them, purposeful enough to want to modernize their societies, and efficient enough to have some ideas about how to do it. Whether such governments are capitalist or socialist can be of little interest to the people involved, or to anyone except their present rulers, whose prerequisites are at stake, and their great power mentors, fretting in their distant capitols about ideology and "spheres of interest."

I am apprehensive of our ability to stay out of war in Laos and Cambodia as long as we remain at war in Vietnam. The issues in the three countries are inseparable. I do not see how we can get out of any of them except by means of political settlement applying to all of them. As they have shown by their advance in Laos, and as further developments in Cambodia may also demonstrate, the Communists are not going to confine the fight to a battlefield of our choosing and, as Secretary Rogers readily admitted, the initiative is theirs.

I do not know what more is needed to demonstrate the incongruity of the policy of Vietnamization. The Administration is trying to strike a "low posture" in the rest of Southeast Asia while preserving an American base in Vietnam, and the Communists are not allowing them to do it. They cannot drive us out of Indochina, but they can force upon us the choice of either plunging in altogether or getting out altogether.

It is this choice that the Nixon Administration has thus far refused to make. "Myth" is a mild word for madness on so grand a scale. Not only has the rationale for Vietnam proved unfounded; it has shown itself to be disastrously mistaken. Instead of deterring Communist intervention in Southeast Asia, American military involvement has turned out to be a powerful   magnet for it.

RESEARCHER CHARGES THIEU RUNS DRUG TRADE

A narcotics researcher charged Friday that South Vietnam's president, former vice-president and prime minister run organizations that control their nation's opium and heroin trade.

The researcher, Alfred W. McCoy, said in Senate testimony that the South Vietnam narcotics ring has links with Corsican gangsters, with an organized-crime family in Florida and with scores of high-ranking military officers in South Vietnam, Laos, Cambodia and Thailand.

McCoy, a Ph.D. candidate in Southeast Asian history at Yale University, testified before the Senate Appropriations Committee's subcommittee on foreign operations. He said that he had spent 18 months interviewing officials in the United States, Indochina and Europe.

McCoy accused American officials of condoning and even cooperating with corrupt elements in Southeast Asia's illegal drug trade out of political and military considerations,

"Senators Told Thieu and Ky Run Drug Trade," Associated Press. (Reprinted from the **Minneapolis Tribune**, June 3, 1972, p. 2A.)

We have one great liability and one great asset for negotiating a political settlement. The liability is our peculiar devotion to the Saigon dictators. Since they survive at our sufferance, the handicap could be removed by the simple expedient of putting Mr. Theiu and Mr. Ky on notice that they can either join us in negotiating a compromise peace or make some arrangement of their own. Of all the options open to the Thieu government, the only one we can and should remove is their present veto on American policy.

"PRESIDENT THIEU IS INTERESTED ONLY IN PROVIDING THE AMERICAN PEOPLE WITH THE TRUTH ABOUT THESE SUICIDES, MISTER AMBASSADOR!"

Ollie Harrington in the **Daily World**, July 28, 1973

I have always been puzzled by our gratuitous tenderheartedness toward rightwing dictators who need us far more than we need them. It is one thing to tolerate such regimes, because it is not our business to be overthrowing foreign governments anyway. But in the case of such unsavory military dictatorships as those in Greece and South Vietnam, we have been much more than tolerant; we have aided and supported these regimes against their own internal enemies. I do not think this is done out of softheartedness — although our Embassy in Saigon has seemed extravagantly solicitous of Mr. Thieu, even to the extent that Ambassador Bunker has staunchly refused to intercede on behalf of Tran Ngoc Chau, the South Vietnamese deputy who was sentenced by a kangaroo court to 10 years at hard labor for maintaining contacts with his brother, a North Vietnamese agent — despite the fact that Chau reported these contacts to the CIA and the US Embassy.

It takes more than Realpolitik to explain such gratuitous friendliness toward rightwing dictators. I suspect that the explanation lies in that attitude of crusading anticommunism which has colored so much of American foreign policy over the years. The charm of the rightwing dictators has been their staunch anticommunism, and that appears to have been enough to compensate for such trivial defects as their despotism and corruption... If devotion to Thieu and Ky are the obstacle to a compromise political settlement, the asset we have is our remaining force of over 400,000 men in Vietnam — and our freedom to take them out. The Communists want them out, and it is supremely in our interest to get them out. That would seem a promising basis for doing business.

THE CASE FOR VIETNAMIZATION

Richard M. Nixon

Richard M. Nixon won the presidential elections of 1968 and 1972. He served as President from his inauguration in January of 1969 to the date of his resignation on August 8, 1974.

Think of the following questions while you read:

1. Why did President Nixon say the U.S. intervened militarily in Vietnam?
2. What did he say had been the main obstacle to a negotiated settlement in Vietnam?
3. How did President Nixon describe and justify his policy of Vietnamization?

President Richard M. Nixon in a speech delivered on Vietnam to a national radio and television audience on November 3, 1969. Reprinted from hearings before the Senate Committee on Foreign Relations on November 18 and 19, 1969.

Good evening, my fellow Americans:

Tonight I want to talk to you on a subject of deep concern to all Americans ànd to many people in all parts of the world — the war in Vietnam.

I believe that one of the reasons for the deep division about Vietnam is that many Americans have lost confidence in what their government has told them about our policy. The American people cannot and should not be asked to support a policy which involves the over-riding issues of war and peace unless they know the truth about that policy....

Fifteen years ago North Vietnam, with the logistical support of Communist China and the Soviet Union, launched a campaign to impose a Communist government on South Vietnam by instigating and supporting a revolution.

In response to the request of the government of South Vietnam, President Eisenhower sent economic aid and military equipment to assist the people of South Vietnam in their efforts to prevent a Communist takeover. Seven years ago, President Kennedy sent 16,000 military personnel to Vietnam as combat advisors. Four years ago, President Johnson sent American combat forces to South Vietnam....

For these reasons, I rejected the recommendation that I should end the war by immediately withdrawing all our forces. I chose instead to change American policy on both the negotiating front and the battle-front....

It has become clear that the obstacle in negotiating an end to the war is not the President of the United States. And it is not the South Vietnamese.

The obstacle is the other side's absolute refusal to show the least willingness to join us in seeking a just peace. It will not do so while it is convinced that all it has to do is to wait for our next concession, and the next until it gets everything it wants.

There can now be no longer any question that progress in negotiation depends only on Hanoi's deciding to negotiate, to negotiate seriously.

I realize that this report on our efforts on the diplomatic fronts is discouraging to the American people, but the American people are entitled to know the truth — the bad news as well as the good news, where the lives of our young men are involved.

Now let me turn, however, to a more encouraging report on another front.

At the time we launched our search for peace I recognized we might not succeed in bringing an end to the war through negotiation. I, therefore, put into effect another plan to bring peace — a plan which will bring the war to an end regardless of what happens on the negotiating front.

It is in line with a major shift in U.S. foreign policy which I described in my press conference at Guam on July 25. Let me briefly explain what has been described as the Nixon Doctrine — a policy which not only will help end the war in Vietnam, but which is an essential element of our program to prevent future Vietnams.

We Americans are a do-it-yourself people. We are an impatient people. Instead of teaching someone else to do a job, we like to do it ourselves. And this trait has been carried over into our foreign policy.

In Korea and again in Vietnam, the United States furnished most of the money, most of the arms, and most of the men to help the people of those countries defend their freedom against the Communist aggression.

Before any American troops were committed to Vietnam, a leader of another Asian country expressed this opinion to me when I was traveling in Asia as a private citizen. He said, ''When you are trying to assist another nation defend its freedom, U.S. policy should be to help them fight the war but not to fight the war for them.''

Well, in accordance with this wise counsel, I laid down in Guam three principles as guidelines for future American policy toward Asia:

First, the United States will keep all of its treaty commitments.

Second, we shall provide a shield if a nuclear power threatens the freedom of a nation allied with us or of a nation whose survival we consider vital to our security.

Third, in cases involving other types of aggression, we shall furnish military and economic assistance when requested in accordance with our treaty commitments. But we shall look to the nation directly threatened to assume the primary responsibility of providing the manpower for its defense.

After I announced this policy, I found that the leaders of the Philippines, Thailand, Vietnam, South Korea, and other nations which might be threatened by Communist aggression, welcomed this new direction in American foreign policy.

The defense of freedom is everybody's business — not just America's business. And it is particularly the responsibility of the people whose freedom is threatened. In the previous Administration, we Americanized the war in Vietnam. In this Administration, we are Vietnamizing the search for peace.

The policy of the previous Administration not only resulted in our assuming the primary responsibility for fighting the war but even more significantly did not adequately stress the goal of strengthening the South Vietnamese so that they could defend themselves when we left.

The Vietnamization Plan was launched following Secretary Laird's visit to Vietnam in March. Under the plan, I ordered first a substantial increase in the training and equipment of South Vietnamese forces.

In July, on my visit to Vietnam, I changed General Abrams' orders so that they were consistent with the objectives of our new policies. Under the new orders, the primary mission of our troops is to enable the South Vietnamese forces to assume the full responsibility for the security of South Vietnam.

Our air operations have been reduced by over 20 percent.

And now we have begun to see the results of this long overdue change in American policy in Vietnam.

VIETNAMIZATION
IS BEST FOR U.S.

Vietnamization of the war. This is the policy adopted by my government, which I support, under present conditions.

When I was the commander in Korea, I visited the French then fighting in Vietnam. I urged them to start a training program for the South Vietnamese, similar to the successful one we were using for Koreans. This was not accepted.

The best way for the United States to extricate itself from Vietnam with honor is to train the South Vietnam army and to equip it with modern weapons.

As these troops assume responsibilities which are now ours, our soldiers should be brought home as the military situation permits, remembering that we still have 50,000 troops in Korea 17 years after the armistice.

General Mark W. Clark in a **New York Times** article, ''Why Vietnamization Is Best.'' (Reprinted in the **Minneapolis Tribune**, February 23, 1970.)

After five years of Americans going into Vietnam, we are finally bringing American men home. By December 15, over 60,000 men will have been withdrawn from South Vietnam — including 20 percent of all of our combat forces.

The South Vietnamese have continued to gain in strength. As a result they have been able to take over combat responsibilities from our American troops.

Two other significant developments have occurred since this Administration took office.

Enemy infiltration, infiltration which is essential if they are to launch a major attack, over the last three months is less than 20 percent of what it was over the same period last year.

Most important — United States casualties have declined during the last two months to the lowest point in three years.

Let me now turn to our program for the future.

We have adopted a plan which we have worked out in cooperation with the South Vietnamese for the complete withdrawal of all U.S. combat ground forces, and their replacement by South Vietnamese forces on an orderly scheduled timetable. This withdrawal will be made from strength and not from weakness. As South Vietnamese forces become stronger, the rate of American withdrawal can become greater.

I have not and do not intend to announce the timetable for our program. There are obvious reasons for this decision which I am sure you will understand. As I have indicated on several occasions, the rate of withdrawal will depend on developments on three fronts.

One of these is the progress which can be or might be made in the Paris talks. An announcement of a fixed timetable for our withdrawal would completely remove any incentive for the enemy to negotiate an agreement.

They would simply wait until our forces had withdrawn and then move in.

The other two factors on which we will base our withdrawal decisions are the level of enemy activity and the progress of the training program of the South Vietnamese forces. I am glad to be able to report tonight progress on both of these fronts has been greater than we anticipated when we started the program in June for withdrawal. As a result, our timetable for withdrawal is more optimistic now than when we made our first estimates in June. This clearly demonstrates why it is not wise to be frozen in on a fixed timetable.

We must retain the flexibility to base each withdrawal decision on the situation as it is at that time rather than on estimates that are no longer valid.

Along with this optimistic estimate, I must — in all candor — leave one note of caution.

If the level of enemy activity significantly increases we might have to adjust our timetable accordingly.

However, I want the record to be completely clear on one point.

At the time of the bombing halt just a year ago, there was some confusion as to whether there was an understanding on the part of the enemy that if we stopped the bombing of North Vietnam they would stop the shelling of cities in South Vietnam. I want to be sure that there is no misunderstanding on the part of the enemy with regard to our withdrawal program.

We have noted the reduced level of infiltration, the reduction of our casualties, and are basing our withdrawal decisions partially on those factors.

If the level of infiltration or our casualties increase while we are trying to scale down the fighting, it will be the result of a conscious decision by the enemy.

Hanoi could make no greater mistake than to assume that an increase in violence will be to its advantage. If I conclude that increased enemy action jeopardizes our remaining forces in Vietnam, I shall not hesitate to take strong and effective measures to deal with that situation.

This is not a threat. This is a statement of policy which as Commander-in-Chief of our Armed Forces I am making in meeting my responsibility for the protection of American fighting men wherever they may be.

My fellow Americans, I am sure you recognize from what I have said that we really only have two choices open to us if we want to end this war.

I can order an immediate, precipitate withdrawal of all Americans from Vietnam without regard to the effects of that action.

Or we can persist in our search for a just peace through a negotiated settlement if possible, or through continued implementation of our plan for Vietnamization if necessary — a plan in which we will withdraw all of our forces from Vietnam on a schedule in accordance with our program, as the South Vietnamese become strong enough to defend their own freedom.

I have chosen the second course.

It is not the easy way.

It is the right way.

It is a plan which will end the war and serve the cause of peace — not just in Vietnam but in the Pacific and in the world.

In speaking of the consequences of a precipitate withdrawal, I mentioned that our allies would lose confidence in America.

Far more dangerous, we would lose confidence in ourselves. The immediate reaction would be a sense of relief that our men were coming home. But as we saw the consequences of what we had done, inevitable remorse and divisive recrimination would scar our spirit as a people.

We have faced other crises in our history and have become stronger by rejecting the easy way out and taking the right way in meeting our challenges. Our greatness as a nation has been our capacity to do what had to be done when we knew our course was right.

THE CASE AGAINST VIETNAMIZATION

George S. McGovern

George S. McGovern is a Democratic Senator from South Dakota. Senator McGovern was defeated by Richard M. Nixon in the presidential election of 1972. Senator McGovern was one of the first Congressional critics of American military intervention in South Vietnam.

Consider the following questions while reading:

1. How does Senator McGovern describe the Saigon Government of General Thieu?
2. What solution to the war does he advocate?
3. Why is Senator McGovern opposed to President Nixon's policy of Vietnamization?
4. How do you interpret the cartoon in this reading?

George S. McGovern in a statement during hearings before the Senate Committee on Foreign Relations on February 4, 1970.

Mr. Chairman, and members of the committee, the resolution that I have submitted with the cosponsorship of Senators Church, Cranston, Goodell, Hughes, McCarthy, Moss, Nelson, Ribicoff, and Young of Ohio calls for the withdrawal from Vietnam of all U.S. forces, the pace to be limited only by these three considerations: the safety of our troops during the withdrawal process, the mutual release of prisoners of war, and arrangements for asylum in friendly countries for any Vietnamese who might feel endangered by our disengagement. (I have recently been advised by the Department of Defense that the 484,000 men we now have in Vietnam could be transported to the United States at a total cost of $144,519,621.)

This process of orderly withdrawal could be completed, I believe, in less than a year's time.

U.S. Support of Saigon Regime is Major Barrier to Peace

Such a policy of purposeful disengagement is the only appropriate response to the blunt truth that there will be no resolution of the war so long as we cling to the Thieu-Ky regime. That government has no dependable political base other than the American military presence and it will never be accepted either by its challengers in South Vietnam or in Hanoi.

We can continue to pour our blood and substance into a neverending effort to support the Saigon hierarchy or we can have peace, but we cannot have both General Thieu and an end to the war.

Our continued military embrace of the Saigon regime is the major barrier, both to peace in Southeast Asia and to the healing of our own society. It assures that the South Vietnamese generals will take no action to build a truly representative government which can either compete with the NLF or negotiate a settlement of the war. It deadlocks the Paris negotiations and prevents the scheduling of serious discussions on the release and exchange of prisoners of war. It diverts our energies and resources from critical domestic needs. It sends young Americans to be maimed or killed in a war that we cannot win and that will not end so long as our forces are there in support of General Thieu.

----from **Herblock's State Of The Union** (Simon & Schuster, 1972)

I have long believed that there can be no settlement of the Vietnam struggle until some kind of provisional coalition government assumes control in Saigon. But

23

this is precisely what General Thieu will never consider. After the Midway conference last June he said, "I solemnly declare that there will be no coalition government, no peace cabinet, no transitional government, not even a reconciliatory government."

Although President Nixon has placed General Thieu as one of the two or three greatest statesmen of our age, Thieu has brushed off the suggestion that he broaden his government and has denounced those who advocate or suggest a negotiated peace as pro-Communist racketeers and traitors. A coalition government means death, he has said.

Mr. Chairman, let us not delude ourselves. This is a clear prescription for an endless war, and changing its name to Vietnamization still leaves us tied to a regime that cannot successfully wage war or make peace.

When administration officials expressed the view that American combat forces might be out of Vietnam by the end of 1970, General Thieu called a press conference last month and insisted that this was an "impossible and impractical goal" and that instead withdrawal "will take many years."

U.S. Vietnamization Policy

And yet there is wide currency to the view that America's course in Southeast Asia is no longer an issue, that the policy of Vietnamization promises an early end of hostilities. That is a false hope emphatically contradicted not only by our ally in Saigon but by the tragic lessons of the past decade.

As I understand the proposal, Vietnamization directs the withdrawal of American troops only as the Saigon armed forces demonstrate their ability to take over the war. Yet a preponderance of evidence indicates that the Vietnamese people do not feel the Saigon regime is worth fighting for. Without local support, "Vietnamization" becomes a plan for the permanent deployment of American combat troops, and not a strategy for disengagement. The President has created a fourth branch of the American Government by giving Saigon a veto over American foreign policy.

If we follow our present policy in Vietnam, there will still be an American Army in my opinion, of 250,000 or 300,000 men in Southeast Asia 15 or 20 years hence or perhaps indefinitely. Meanwhile American firepower and bombardment will have killed more tens of thousands of Vietnamese who want nothing other than an end of the war. All this to save a corrupt, unrepresentative regime in Saigon.

Any military escalation by Hanoi or the Vietcong would pose a challenge to American forces which would require heavier American military action and, therefore, heavier American casualties, or we would be faced with the possibility of a costly, forced withdrawal.

ASIAN WARS WOULD DRAIN U.S. RESOURCES

Under pressure from hawks like Nixon, John Foster Dulles and Admiral Radford, Eisenhower laid the seeds of future trouble by setting up the Diem regime in the South and encouraging it to refuse elections two years later. But Ike did resist American intervention. At a White House conference on whether to intervene rather than accept the Geneva settlement, Eisenhower observed "that if the U.S. were unilaterally to permit its forces to be drawn into conflict in Indochina and in a succession of Asian wars, the end result would be to drain off our resources and to weaken our overall defense situation." That is exactly what the Vietnamese war has done, and what its continuation under Nixon will continue to do.

I. F. Stone, "The Old Nixon Surfaces Again," **I. F. Stone's Weekly**, November 17, 1969, p. 1.

The Vietnamization policy is based on the same false premises which have doomed to failure our previous military efforts in Vietnam. It assumes that the Thieu-Ky regime in Saigon stands for freedom and a popularly backed regime. Actually, the Saigon regime is an oppressive dictatorship which jails its critics and blocks the development of a broadly based government. Last June 20, the Saigon minister for liaison for parliament, Von Huu Thu, confirmed that 34,540 political prisoners were being held and that many of those people were non-Communists who were guilty of nothing more than advocating a neutral peaceful future for their country. In proportion to population the political prisoners held by Saigon would be the equivalent of a half million political prisoners in the United States.

The Thieu-Ky regime is no closer to American ideals than its challenger, the National Liberation Front. Indeed self-determination and independence are probably far stronger among the Vietnamese guerrillas and their supporters than within the Saigon Government camp.

I have never felt that American interests and ideals were represented by the Saigon generals or their corrupt predecessors. We should cease our embrace of this regime now and cease telling the American people that it stands for freedom.

Opposition To U.S. Vietnamization Policy

I should like to make clear that I am opposed to both the principle and the practice of the policy of Vietnamization. I am opposed to the policy, whether it works by the standard of its proponents or does not work. I oppose as immoral and self-defeating a policy which gives either American arms or American blood to perpetuate a corrupt and unrepresentative foreign regime. It is not in the interests of either the American or the Vietnamese people to maintain such a government.

I find it morally and politically repugnant for us to create a client group of Vietnamese generals in Saigon and then give them murderous military technology to turn against their own people.

Vietnamization is basically an effort to tranquilize the conscience of the American people while our Government wages a cruel and needless war by proxy.

An enlightened American foreign policy would cease

trying to dictate the outcome of an essentially local struggle involving various groups of Vietnamese. If we are concerned about a future threat to Southeast Asia from China, let us have the commonsense to recognize that a strong independent regime even though organized by the National Liberation Front and Hanoi would provide a more dependable barrier tò Chinese imperialism than the weak puppet regime we have kept in power at the cost of 40,000 American lives and hundreds of thousands of Vietnamese lives.

Even if we could remove most of our forces from Vietnam, how could we justify before God and man the use of our massive firepower to continue a slaughter that neither serves our interests nor the interests of the Vietnamese.

The policy of Vietnamization is a cruel hoax designed to screen from the American people the bankruptcy of a needless military involvement in the affairs of the Vietnamese people. Instead of Vietnamizing the war let us encourage the Vietnamization of the government in South Vietnam. We can do that by removing the embrace that now prevents other political groups from assuming a leadership role in Saigon, groups that are capable of expressing the desire for peace of the Vietnamese people.

UNDERSTANDING STEREOTYPES

A stereotype is an oversimplified or exaggerated description. It can apply to things or people and be favorable or unfavorable. Quite often stereotyped beliefs about racial, religious, and national groups are insulting and oversimplified. They are usually based on misinformation or lack of information.

The Thunderbolt, February 1, 1975

Muhammed Speaks, April 18, 1975

PART I

The cartoons above are examples of stereotyping. Examine the cartoons carefully and, with other class members, discuss why they are examples of stereotyping.

PART II

Read through the following list carefully. Mark **S** for any statement that is an example of stereotyping. Mark **N** for any statement that is not an example of stereotyping. Mark **U** if you are undecided about any statement. Then discuss and compare your decisions with other class members.

S = Stereotype
N = Not a stereotype
U = Undecided

_____1. Asia consists of a wide range of landscapes and climatic regions.

_____2. African people are largely primitive and backward.

_____3. Asia is a land of diversity.

_____4. The Japanese are masters at copying Western technology.

_____5. Asian countries are poor and underdeveloped.

_____6. Racial conflict is a problem in many societies.

_____7. Most Jews are wealthy people.

_____8. Inflation is especially hard on poor people.

_____9. Black people are poor and lack education.

_____10. Chinese Americans are energetic people.

_____11. Indians have made many contributions to the American heritage.

_____12. The Vietnamese do not value life as highly as most Americans.

CAMBODIAN INCURSION WILL SHORTEN WAR

John Tower

John Tower is a Republican Senator from Texas. He was a leading conservative spokesman in support of President Nixon's policy in Vietnam.

Bring the following questions to your reading:

1. Why does Senator Tower say the Cambodian operation was a military success?
2. How does he describe the performance of the South Vietnamese Army?
3. What role does he think Congress should play in our nation's policy in Indochina?

John Tower, ''Cambodia: Two Views,'' **St. Paul Pioneer Press**, June 14, 1970, pp. 1, 10. Reprinted by permission of The Associated Press Newsfeatures.

The recent operation of U.S. and South Vietnamese troops inside the border areas of Cambodia where the enemy formerly enjoyed sanctuary has been an unqualified military success.

The operation has demonstrated that the Vietnamization program, designed to enable us to eventually remove our combat forces from South Vietnam, is progressing at an even more rapid rate than I had imagined. The operation has undoubtedly hastened the time when our objective of attaining an honorable peace can be achieved.

I arrived at these conclusions after visiting combat zones in Cambodia and South Vietnam as a member of the Presidential Task Force which toured the area a week ago.

I saw many of the weapons and much of the ammunition, food and communications equipment which our Cambodian operation has denied the enemy. The amount of this captured war material is so great that I do not believe the enemy will be capable of mounting any sustained main force engagement in the Third and Fourth Corps tactical areas of South Vietnam for some time.

In my discussions with our troops, I found the morale of our fighting men high, as morale generally is among troops who are maintaining the initiative against an enemy. I learned also from former enemy combatants who have recently defected that the Cambodian operation has had a demoralizing effect upon the enemy.

The Cambodian operation was the first time in which the South Vietnamese themselves were responsible for a massive offensive operation involving all elements of their armed services. They executed their operation efficiently, courageously and professionally. They demonstrated a fast-growing capability to carry on future combat roles without U.S. combat assistance.

Our action to deny the enemy unrestricted sanctuary; to deny him the use of vast quantities of war material; to demonstrate allied capability to strike when we desire; to demonstrate our determination to attain an honorable peace; to demonstrate the capability of the army of South Vietnam who work together toward the attainment of lasting peace. Time is now on our side. We need not surrender through immediate withdrawal and thereby relinquish world influence.

Because I have returned from the Task Force tour with increased optimism, I am all the more opposed to any action by the Congress which might restrict the President's capability as commander in chief. I believe the commander in chief must have the power to execute military operations as required by situational developments.

ADVISE AND CONSENT

I would say, yes, we can exercise our advise and consent function, because the exercise of that function does not require that the Senate know the innermost intelligence planning of the Office of the Commander in Chief and of its agencies.

The President has made it clear to the public, has made it clear to me in conversation, that he does have a plan, and that he has always qualified it, as the Senator knows, by saying that some aspects of that plan are conditioned on three criteria he has often enunciated.

I think if the plan were made known to the Senate, a risk would have to be taken that it would be made known to the public, therefore to Hanoi and, therefore, if Hanoi were aware of our timetable, it would be in an excellent position to counter every move we make that is designed to produce a peaceful result.

Senator Hugh Scott in a statement during hearings before the Senate Committee on Foreign Relations of February 4, 1970.

To be effective, military operations must often be executed rapidly. To insure their success, we cannot tell the enemy of our strategic plans.

If the commander in chief were forced to discuss detailed military plans with the Congress, any forthcoming public debate would slow our ability to act and would inform the enemy of our intentions. Restrictions placed upon the options of the commander in chief serve to provide guarantees for the enemy.

I know that all Americans are tired of the war in Southeast Asia. I know the Congress and the administration is tired of the war. I am tired of the war. But I believe that most Americans would like to extricate ourselves in a manner which will encourage a stable peace. We should not leave a vacuum to be filled by Communists.

We must follow a responsible course. Vietnamization is such a course. I am convinced that the Cambodian operation has helped hasten Vietnamization and has helped to insure its success.

CAMBODIAN INVASION WILL WIDEN WAR

Walter F. Mondale

Walter F. Mondale is a Democratic Senator from Minnesota. He became a leading Senate critic of American policy in Vietnam during the Nixon Presidency.

Use the following questions to assist you in your reading:

1. According to Senator Mondale, what objective was President Nixon seeking in Vietnam?
2. How did he view the Vietnamization policy?
3. Why was Senator Mondale opposed to the invasion of Cambodia?
4. Can you relate the cartoon in this reading to any comments by Senator Mondale?

Walter F. Mondale in a speech before the national convention of the Americans for Democratic Action. (Reprinted from the **Congressional Record**, May 19, 1970.)

I had been trying to decide what my topic — our keynote — should be. The President's speech last night settled the question for all of us.

There is only one. The war which *was* in Vietnam and which *was* — if slowly — being wound down, is now in Indochina and is now being massively escalated.

The war which has cost:

Some 50,000 American lives;

Almost 275,000 American wounded;

Unknown millions of Vietnamese casualties;

Some 100 billion dollars worth of our resources; and

A decade of agony and strife at home...has now become an even deeper and wider war.

"Vietnamization" has now been fully revealed for a tragic hoax.

Many of us feared that Vietnamization was largely a device to buy time and pre-exempt dissent while propping up the corrupt regime of Thieu and Ky. But many of us also felt that the President, if for no other reason than politics, was committed to "winding down" the war in Vietnam.

It is now clear that the President has not abandoned the disastrous objective of the last tragic decade. It is *military victory* that he seeks — the perpetuation of whatever anticommunist government can be found, — however corrupt, unpopular, or undemocratic, and however little they will fight to defend themselves, by whatever military means are necessary. It is a policy which seeks to preserve an American bridgehead on the Mainland of Southeast Asia.

This is the *old* policy. It is a policy which has been shown to be unattainable, irrational, unpopular at home and abroad, and contrary to American interests.

The invasion of the Cambodian sanctuaries is in direct contradiction of the President's own Guam Doctrine, in which he said that we must cease acting as policeman and cannon fodder for the Asian nations. It is in direct contradiction of the interpretation of "Vietnamization" which the President has given to the American people. It is, in fact, absolute proof of the total failure of the "Vietnamization" doctrine.

We cannot have it both ways. We cannot have both disengagement and escalation. We cannot hold to a goal of peace, disengagement, and a "political solution" while expanding the war and seeking the total destruction of the enemy.

Copyright, **Los Angeles Times**
Reprinted with permission

The rationale is the same one we heard 10 years and 50,000 lives ago: "A little more effort and the tide will be turned." We have heard it often since — a few thousand more troops, a little more bombing and the war will be over.

Now we are told that a six to eight week foray into Cambodia will wipe out the major communist sanctuaries and staging areas which they have held for at least the last five years.

But why weren't we told 6 months ago that "Vietnamization" would require the invasion of these territories which have been held by the communists for so many years?

Why weren't we told a week ago when the President reported sufficient success to announce the pull out of 150,000 more troops in the year ahead?

What do we expect the Vietcong, the North Vietnamese — and the Chinese and the Soviets, for that matter — to do while we destroy their major supply and staging areas?

What will we do in 2 months when, if all goes exactly as planned, we will have pushed them out of the Parrot's Beak, the Fish Hook, and the other areas? Do we stay there...indefinitely...or do we return to South Vietnam and expect *them* to stay wherever we may have been lucky enough to have pushed them?

How about the next line of communist sanctuaries — just beyond the reach of American forces? All of Asia behind the enemy line is a "sanctuary." When and where do we stop? And when do they decide to attack our own sanctuaries — at Thailand, for example?

The President's reason for this escalation must be rejected. There is no way to make a "defensive maneuver" out of a full scale offensive into a neutral nation, with the advice and consent neither of that nation nor of Congress.

There is no way to make this escalation into a means of "hastening our withdrawal" or "furthering a political settlement."

38

THIS IS NOT AN INVASION

"This is not an invasion of Cambodia." So Richard Nixon said on April 30, 1970, announcing that American troops were entering Cambodia to "clean out" enemy sanctuaries. He spoke of how "scrupulously" the United States had theretofore respected Cambodia neutrality. He said he had no intention of "expanding the war into Cambodia."

But American planes had in fact been bombing Cambodia for 14 months, the targets concealed by an elaborate system of false reporting. And of course Cambodia was then dragged into full-scale war, lately including some of the heaviest bombing in history.

And the lies went on.

Anthony Lewis, "America: An Arrogant, Lawless Giant?" New York Times Service. (Reprinted in the **Minneapolis Tribune**, August 14, 1973, p. 4A.)

The oldest myth of them all again rears its destructive head: the notion of a monolithic world-wide communist conspiracy unalterably committed to the conquest of the world — a conspiracy which must be stopped at whatever cost — "so that the sons and brothers of our soldiers fighting now can live in peace and security!"

One of the tragic ironies of the war, of course, is that the Administration still clings at the same time to the *hope* that we can achieve our ends without a total military commitment...that we can ultimately gain from a conference table what we failed to gain on the battlefield....

I now see a longer war and a wider war. I see many more deaths. I think we should know by this time the patience, resolve, and manpower of the Vietcong and

39

the North Vietnamese. And I see us now sinking further and further into a wider, more disastrous, more unwinable, and even more unjustifiable war....

I am deeply disturbed at the thought of a generation which may lose all confidence in the ability of a democracy to respond with justice, reason, and humanity. But what can we expect of a generation which is asked to kill and be killed in a war which cannot be explained? Can a fractured, disheartened and demoralized America possibly be a price worth paying for a few more years of an Americanized government in Saigon, and in Phnom Penh?

Perhaps the greatest crime of this war is that we have forced young men and women to choose between these two instincts. The great majority of the young will never feel a bullet or a piece of shrapnel. But nearly all will be called upon to disavow either their conscience, or their country.

The President said "we will not be humiliated." But we already are.

I believe the highest and noblest expression of civilized manhood is to admit error when one is wrong. The same must be true of Nations.

If we did, it would indeed be "our finest hour." — It would be the President's final hour.

We could deal with our *real* problems: in the Middle East, in Vienna, in the Ghettos, on Indian Reservations, in migrant camps, in our schools and hospitals and churches. We could save our oceans, lakes and streams and our air. We could reclaim our streets and assault crime without sacrificing justice. We might reclaim our young, increasing numbers of whom have tragically rejected the institutions and the processes of freedom. This Nation might even reclaim its soul.

VIETNAM AND THE DEFENSE OF FREEDOM

Thomas J. Dodd

Thomas J. Dodd served as a Democratic Senator from Connecticut. He was a supporter of President Lyndon B. Johnson's Vietnam policy.

Keep the following questions in mind while you read:

1. How did Senator Dodd define what he called ''the new isolationism?''
2. Why did he say that the U.S. should not withdraw from Vietnam?
3. What did Senator Dodd say were the key elements in the defense of the ''free world?''
4. What do you think he meant by the term ''free world?'' How would you define the term?

Thomas J. Dodd in a Senate speech on February 23, 1965.

There has been developing in this country in recent years a brand of thinking about foreign affairs which, I believe, can aptly be described as "the new isolationism." This internal phenomenon is, in my opinion, potentially more disastrous in terms of its consequence than the major external problems that confront us.

Its background is a growing national weariness with Cold War burdens we have been so long carrying, a rising frustration with situations that are going against us in many places, a long-simmering indignation over the fact that our generosity and sacrifice have too often been met abroad, not just with indifference and ingratitude, but even with hostility and contempt.

Its political base seems to be to the Left of center, although it forms as yet a distinct minority there.

Its scareword is "escalation"; its cure-all is "neutralization."

Its prophets include some of my colleagues in the Congress, influential spokesmen in the press, and leading figures in the academic world. Some are new volunteers in this cause of retrenchment; they regard themselves as pragmatists. Others are old hands at Pollyanna-ism, those unshakable romantics who were disillusioned by Moscow at the time of the Hitler-Stalin pact, disillusioned by Mao when they discovered that he was not really an agrarian reformer, disillusioned by Castro when they learned that he was not a cross between Thomas Jefferson and Robin Hood — and who, having again dusted themselves off, now look for new vistas of adventure....

The basic premise of the new isolationism is that the United States is overextended in its attempt to resist Communist aggression around the world, overcommitted to the defense of distant outposts, and overinvolved in the murky and unintelligible affairs of remote areas.

The corollaries of the new isolationism are many. It is contended that we should de-emphasize the Cold War and reverse our national priorities in favor of domestic improvements; that we should withdraw from South Viet-Nam; that we should cease involvement in the Congo; that we should relax the so-called rigidity of our Berlin policy; that foreign aid has outlived its use-fulness and should be severely cut back; that our Military Establishment and our C.I.A. organizations that seem particularly suspect because they are symbols of world-wide involvement, should be humbled and "cut down to size" and stripped of their influence in foreign policy questions.

Editorial cartoon by Lou Grant of the **Oakland Tribune**
Copyright, Los Angeles Times Syndicate
Reprinted with permission

In my judgment all of these propositions have one thing in common. Each of them would strike at the heart of our national effort to preserve our freedom and our security; and collectively they add up to a policy which I can describe by no other name than "appeasement," subtle appeasement, unintentional appeasement, to be sure, but appeasement nonetheless.

My purpose, this afternoon then, is to oppose these propositions and to enlist Senators' opposition against them — for the new isolationism is as bankrupt as the old.

First of all — to tackle the main premise — I reject the assumption that the United States is overextended, or overcommitted, or overinvolved.

We are enjoying a spectacular growth in every index of national strength. Our population, our wealth, our industrial capacity, our scientific potential, our agricultural output, all are enjoying great upward surges. We were informed that our Gross National Product was again up in January, and the trend seems ever upward.

Far from overextending ourselves in the Cold War, we are actually in a period of declining defense budgets, of steadily lowered draft calls, of sharply reduced foreign aid, of one tax cut after another.

Let me emphasize this: In every basic resource, we have greater capacity today than during the past five years; by every military or economic standard, we are stronger; and by every physical measurement, the percentage of our resources going into the Cold War is lower. Why then should we talk of weariness or overcommitment?

We are not even straining ourselves. We are actually pursuing today a policy not only of both guns and butter, but of less guns and more butter.

So far as our resources go, we are capable of indefinite continuation and even intensification of our present efforts, if need be. It is only our mental, and perhaps our moral, resources which seem to be feeling the strain.

44

We would, of course, prefer to live in a world in which it were possible for us to have no commitments, a world in which we could devote all of our energies to the task of perfecting our society at home and enriching the lives of our people.

But we must face the world as it is. And the basic fact of our world is that Western civilization, itself terribly rent and divided, both politically and philosophically, has been forced into a twilight war of survival by a relentless and remorseless enemy.

A SHOWCASE FOR DEMOCRACY

I think we would have much to gain by setting up Vietnam as a showcase, and using it to promote economic understanding and for psychological warfare, as a real living case in point of what it is possible for a large power to do without stealing the sovereignty of or encroaching upon the independence of a small, newly independent republic.

From a speech by Senator Gale W. McGee of Wyoming delivered in the U.S. Senate on February 9, 1960.

It is incontestable, in terms of people enslaved and nations gobbled up over the past twenty years, that we have not been holding our own. And each year, the world Communist movement is committing more and more of its resources to the task of subjugating our allies, all around the perimeter of freedom.

Against this background it is preposterous to maintain that we should reduce our effort and lessen our commitment to the great struggle of our century.

Yet, according to **Time** magazine, it is the widespread sentiment of the academic world that we have overreached ourselves and ought to pull back. Walter Lippmann, the well-known columnist, for whom I have great respect, says that "the American tide will have to recede."

45

It has been argued that we would be in a "precarious situation" if we were attacked on several fronts. Of course we would, but does anyone believe that we can solve the problem by abandoning our commitments and defensive alliances? Would the loss of these countries be any the less disastrous because they were given up undefended?

On the contrary, if we are not strong enough to honor our commitments today, then we should solve the problem, not by reducing our commitments, but by becoming stronger, and by aiding our allies to become stronger.

The defense of the free world rests on a very delicate balance. The key elements in that balance are American power and American determination. If we lack the power to maintain that balance, then certainly all is lost. If we reveal that we lack the determination, if we, for instance, allow ourselves to be pushed out of Viet-Nam, such a humiliation may indeed be the second shot heard around the world; and a dozen nations might soon throw in the sponge and make whatever accommodation they could with an enemy that would then seem assured of victory.

Fortunately, at the present time we do not lack the power to carry on the defense of freedom. Our power is at its peak and we have the capacity to increase it vastly if necessary. It is our spirit, apparently, that needs shoring up.

Four years ago, after a visit to Southeast Asia, I said on the floor of the Senate:

If the United States, with its unrivaled might, with its unparalleled wealth, with its dominion over sea and air, with its heritage as the champion of freedom — if this United States and its free-world allies have so diminished in spirit that they can be laid in the dust by a few thousand primitive guerrillas, then we are far down the road from which there is no return.

In right and in might, we are able to work our will on this question. Southeast Asia cannot be lost unless we will it to be lost; it cannot be saved unless we will it to be saved.

This problem, seemingly so remote and distant, will in fact be resolved here in the United States, in the Congress, in the administration, and in the minds and hearts of the American people.

46

The passage of four years has not diminished my belief in this course....

Twenty-five years ago, our country, comparatively new and untried among the great nations of the earth, through passage of the Lend-Lease Act, described by Winston Churchill as "the most unsordid act of recorded history," embarked irrevocably upon the path that has brought us to our present posture in history. Through that act, we affirmed the preservation and expansion of liberty as our highest goal; we acknowledged that freedom was insecure everywhere so long as tyranny existed anywhere; and we assumed the burden, and the glory, of being the champion and defender of man's highest aspirations.

Since that embattled hour, when the light of freedom was but a flicker in the dark, our journey across the pages of history has been fantastic and unprecedented: tragic, to be sure, in its mistakes and naïveties, but heroic in its innovations and commitments, prodigious in its energy and power, gigantic in its generosity and good will, noble in its restraint and patience, and sublime in its purpose and in its historic role.

We have not realized the high goals we set for ourselves in World War II.

But we have preserved freedom and national independence in more than half the earth; we have prevented the nuclear holocaust; we have restored Western Europe; we have helped friend and foe to achieve prosperity, freedom and stability; we have launched a world-peace organization and have kept it alive; we have offered the hand of friendship and help to the impoverished and backward peoples of the world if they will but take it.

It may be said of our country today, as of no other in history, that wherever people are willing to stand up in defense of their liberty, Americans stand with them.

We cannot know at this hour whether our journey has just begun or is nearing its climax; whether the task ahead is the work of a generation, or of a century. President Kennedy said, in his Inaugural Address, that the conflict would not be resolved in our lifetime.

The Chief of Staff of the Army recently told the Congress that it might well take ten years to decide the issue in Viet-Nam alone. And Viet-Nam is only one symptom of the disease, the epidemic, we are resisting.

Against this somber background, how foolish it is to talk of de-emphasizing the Cold War, of pulling out of Viet-Nam, of abandoning the Congo to Communist intrigue, of slashing the defense budget by 10 per cent, or of any of the other irresponsibilities of the new isolationism.

READING

VIETNAM AND AMERICAN IMPERIALISM

Sidney Lens

Sidney Lens is a journalist, labor leader and world traveler. He has been an active participant in peace and radical movements. His books include **Radicalism In America**, **The Forging of the American Empire** and **The Labor Wars**.

While reading use the following questions as a guide:

1. Why does Sidney Lens say Vietnams were inevitable?
2. How do you interpret the cartoon in this reading?
3. According to the author, what part did foreign markets play in our Vietnam intervention?
4. What does he mean by the terms **Pax Americana** and ''The American Empire?''

Sidney Lens, ''How It 'Really' All Began,'' **The Progressive**, June, 1973, pp. 20-24. Reprinted by permission from **The Progressive**, 408 West Gorham Street, Madison, Wisconsin 53703. Copyright © 1973, The Progressive, Inc.

It took a number of years before large numbers of people began to realize that Vietnam was no "mistake" but a manifestation of America's global policy, part and parcel of the same policy of intervention and counter-revolution which Washington was practicing around the world....

Given the narrow definition of national interests by the American Establishment — to reshape the world in its own image and for its own purposes — Vietnams were inevitable, whether they occurred in Indochina, or Brazil, or the Dominican Republic, and whether in 1955 or 1965.

Intervention into other peoples' civil wars was not yet an automatic reaction when Acheson made his deal with the French in May, 1950. But it happened more than once and was well on the way to becoming inflexible policy. From 1945 to 1949, Harry Truman had injected himself into the most fateful civil war of all, China, and allocated three billion dollars to support a corrupt, fascist-style dictator, Chiang Kai-shek, in a vain effort to save him from his people. The only difference between China and the future foray in Vietnam was that in China, Washington decided to cut its losses — it was simply impossible to dispatch an army big enough to fight millions of guerrillas in a land of 600 million people.

Even before the Acheson barter arrangement of 1950, President Truman had proclaimed his famous doctrine and supplied the Greek dictatorship with military advisers and hundreds of millions in arms to fight a guerrilla force that, Communist or not, had the people behind it. Subsequently, from 1950 to 1968, America propped up right-of-center regimes in Greece with another billion and a half, to protect them from the horrible alternative that they might establish a democracy. The difference between Greece and Vietnam was that in the former "our side" was able to win without requiring the United States to send its own troops to finish the job....

Why, after all, did a nation that had never spent as much as a billion dollars a year on arms in peacetime suddenly begin appropriating $12 billion, $40 billion, and finally $80 billion annually? To say that it was needed for defense against "Communist aggression" in Europe is pure fiction. The Kremlin, John Foster Dulles conceded in March, 1949, ''does not contemplate the use of war as an instrument of its national policy. I do not know any responsible official, military or civilian, in this government or any government, who believes that the Soviet government now plans conquest by open military aggression.'' The military-industrial complex was fashioned not so much to stop Russian expansion but to advance a vitally-needed American expansion.

"LET'S NOT SPOIL A GOOD THING."

Copyright (C) 1969 The Chicago Sun-Times
Reproduced by courtesy of Wil-Jo Associates, Inc. and Bill Mauldin

"My contention," said Acheson in November, 1944, "is that we cannot have full employment and prosperity in the United States without the foreign markets." Under another system, he argued, "you could use the entire production of the country in the United States," but under capitalism, the Government "must look to foreign markets." There was nothing particularly new about this point; it had been made by American officials as far back as Senator James G. ("Jingo Jim") Blaine in 1881, and reiterated by every administration since Teddy Roosevelt's.

"Since trade ignores national boundaries," wrote historian Woodrow Wilson in 1907, "and the manufacturer insists on having the world as a market, the flag of his nation must follow him, and the doors of the nations which are closed against him must be battered down.... Colonies must be obtained or planted, in order that no useful corner of the world may be overlooked or left unused." Three decades later Franklin Roosevelt proclaimed that "foreign markets must be regained. There is no other way if we would avoid painful economic dislocation, social readjustments, and unemployment." Unless America expanded its markets, said President Franklin Roosevelt's Secretary of Commerce Henry A. Wallace, in his more conservative and official day, the only choices before us would be the unhappy ones of socialism or fascism.

This had been the alpha and omega of U.S. policy ever since America had become a leading industrial nation, and at no time was it more urgently so than in the mid-1940s when industrial capacity had been doubled in the span of a few wartime years. U.S. factories were prepared to produce mountains of goods for a ravaged world if only the world would (a) open its doors to them, and (b) find the wherewithal to pay for them.

The American Establishment solved the dilemma of "ever increasing surpluses" by a combination of foreign aid and militarism. The $149 billion of grants and loans doled out from 1946 through 1971 was given in exchange for economic concession (which only the Communist countries refused to make). Recipient nations had to agree in advance to the "open door" by which American entrepreneurs were permitted to trade

52

and invest in foreign countries on an equal basis with their own nationals, and to the Bretton Woods system by which the dollar became the world's monetary unit, with all the advantages to America that accrue to a banker.

Aid by itself, however, was not sufficient, for to the extent that nations elsewhere refused to join *Pax Americana* or seceded from it, the "free world" and its market potential contracted. The military-industrial complex was fashioned to fill this void, and to assure comformity and loyalty by members of the "free world" consortium.

Those who embrace the "accident" or "personalality" concept of history claim that the military, like Topsy, just grow'd: the generals and admirals insisted on maintaining their status, the anti-Communists and defense manufacturers shouted themselves hoarse for more defense orders. But no nation lavishes one-and-a-third trillion dollars — since 1946 — on a military machine to respond to the whims of its generals, its merchants of death, and its far-our extremists. Postwar American militarism was designed in the first instance to contain the Soviet Union, through deterrence — so that its influence would not upset *Pax Americana* — and to prevent governments and peoples from entertaining ideas of secession from the "American system" through revolution or neutralism.

This, as I see it, was "how it all began" in Vietnam. National interests, as defined by the Establishment, demanded markets and access to raw materials. This in turn demanded a far-flung program of aid, and above all, militarism. At one time or another, the Pentagon trained and supplied weapons to sixty-nine armies, most of them puppet armies ready to do Uncle Sam's bidding and in the process save their own reactionary regimes. It was and is a quid pro quo by which Washington says to such regimes: "We will give you economic aid and military aid to save you from revolutionary wrath in your own countries, in return for which we expect you to be part of the 'American system' and open your doors to Western trade and investment."

That aid, moreover, has its own logic. The $50 or $100 million in grants and training, given to a country

OUR DOLLAR—CROOKED FINGERS

I want to tell you, I don't think the whole of South East Asia, as related to the present and future safety and freedom of the people of this country, is worth the life or limb of a single American. But maybe the people are and maybe the people of South America are, too. And maybe that's confusing.

I believe that if we had and would keep our dirty, bloody, dollar-crooked fingers out of the business of these nations so full of depressed, exploited people, they will arrive at a solution of their own. That they design and want. That they fight and work for. And if unfortunately their revolution must be of the violent type because the "haves" refuse to share with the "have-nots" by any peaceful method, at least what they get will be their own, and not the American style, which they don't want and above all don't want crammed down their throats by Americans.

General David M. Shoup, former Marine Commandant, in a speech delivered on May 14, 1966 at Pierce College in Los Angeles. (Reprinted from hearings before the Senate Committee on Foreign Relations, March 20, 1968, p. 47.)

such as Brazil, is of limited value unless the American Navy — second to none — patrols and controls the seas. It is of limited value without the 3,000-odd U.S. bases and installations around the world from which the Pentagon can quickly move troops into "trouble" areas. And it is almost useless unless there is a large American military force in the background, part of it stationed overseas, ready to intervene when the puppet armies themselves prove inadequate — as they did in Vietnam or the Dominican Republic.

I do not claim there is a one-to-one relationship between American aid and military support on the one hand, and the economic benefits America and its allies can expect. Certainly that is not the case in places like Nicaragua where U.S. investment is negligible but U.S.

54

aid relatively substantial. Washington must consider, in every case, the strategic value of a given nation, as well as the effect of what may happen if that nation turns neutralist or socialist.

Vietnam fits into that category: American investments there were picayune at the time of intervention, but the intervention had strategic import for U.S. influence in the whole area, and it was a stepping stone in addition to expanding the American empire....

The true roots of Vietnam, then, lie in the expanded global interests of the American Establishment after World War II...

Vietnam, then, was no "accident"...It was *the* American policy drawn to its ultimate — and logical — conclusion. Those who still think that it was a "mistake" induced by poor advice are in for further disillusionment as the American leadership continues its policy of buttressing corrupt dictators in Thailand, Brazil, South Vietnam, Cambodia, Taiwan, Bolivia, the Philippines, Malaysia, Nicaragua, and other places. One of them surely will be another Vietnam — unless you and I...mount a vigorous campaign to disarm our military, and to reshape America toward the humanism envisioned by many of our forefathers.

LOCATING SCAPEGOATS

Instructions

The word fascism has emotional and controversial overtones. Scholars often disagree about its meaning. It conjures up images of Hitler, the swastika and Nazi horrors. During their occupation of Europe in the 1940's, the German fascists systematically killed an estimated six million Jews. They continually propagandized the outrageous lie that Jews were responsible for Germany's social ills and problems. Jews became scapegoats of irrational leaders who glorified force, violence, and the doctrines of racial supremacy. The fascists destroyed German democracy by adopting tactics of deceit and propaganda.

One of their principle propaganda weapons was the technique of scapegoating. On an individual level scapegoating involves the mental process of transferring personal blame or anger to another individual or object. Most people, for example, have kicked their table or chair as a psychological outlet for anger and frustration over a mistake or failure. On a social level, this process involves the placement of blame on entire groups of people for social problems that they have not caused. Scapegoats may be totally or only partially innocent, but they always receive more blame than can be rationally justified.

Human societies are so complex that complicated problems are often not completely understood by any citizen. Yet people always demand answers and there exists a human tendency to create imaginary and simplistic explanations for complex racial, social, economic, and political problems that defy easy understanding and solution. In times of great social turmoil, people are more prone to accept the conspiratorial ideas of those who preach hate and unreason. Conspiracy theories of history and causation represent the most dangerous form of scapegoating. This social phenomenon occurs when racial, religious, or ethnic groups are unjustly blamed for serious social problems. This blame can be expressed in terms of verbal and/or overt hatred and aggression. Although scapegoating was a major tactic of the German fascists under Hitler, it is a commonly used technique of contemporary racists and fascists in America. The following activity is designed to help you understand this technique.

"IF YOU PEOPLE HAD MORE ABORTIONS, OUR POLICE WOULD HAVE AN EASIER JOB."

Muhammed Speaks, April 20, 1975

Christian Vanguard, June, 1973

Part I

The above cartoons are examples of scapegoating. Examine the cartoons carefully and, with other class members, discuss why they are examples of scapegoating.

Part II

Read through the following list carefully. Some of the statements are taken from the readings in Chapter Three. Mark **S** for any statement that is an example of scapegoating. Mark **N** for any statement that is not an example of scapegoating. Mark **U** if you are undecided about any statement. Then discuss and compare your decisions with other class members.

> **S = An Example of Scapegoating**
> **N = Not an Example**
> **U = Undecided**

_____1. The profit motive is an important part of the American economy.

_____2. Communists are responsible for most of the world's problems, war and violence.

_____3. Russia is rich in natural resources.

_____4. Many Americans have a high standard of living.

_____5. We must stop the Jews from interfering in our affairs.

_____6. The basic needs of people throughout the world are similar.

_____7. It takes skill and training to become a politician.

_____8. Blacks are largely responsible for the unrest and turmoil in the large American cities.

_____9. Inflation is a serious threat to world economic conditions.

_____10. The white man knows he is the devil and he is steadily on his job, day and night, dividing the black man, turning him against his own black self and kind.

CHAPTER **2**

WHY OUR
POLICY FAILED

THE LIBERAL BETRAYAL OF VIETNAM

Human Events

Human Events is a conservative newsweekly of social and political opinion. National and international problems and issues are dealt with each week by the editors and numerous articles and editorials by other conservative spokesmen appear regularly.

Think of the following questions while you read:

1. According to the editors, how could the American defeat in Vietnam have been prevented?
2. How do the editors say America originally became involved in Vietnam?
3. Who do they say is responsible for the defeat? Why?
4. Can you relate the cartoon in this reading to any ideas expressed by the editors of **Human Events**?

"Why Not Recriminations?" **Human Events**, May 10, 1975, pp. 1, 4. Reprinted with permission.

It is all over now, of course. Virtually all Americans, with an assist from the Soviets (who are so helpful when we're retreating), have been evacuated from South Vietnam. Saigon, now Ho Chi Minh City, is under a Vietcong flag, and the left, both here and abroad, is jubilant.

Encouraged and equipped by Peking and Moscow, Hanoi has inflicted a catastrophic defeat upon the United States. The silver linings are few. The Administration — with zero assistance from the Democratic-controlled Congress which refused to clear any evacuation or aid legislation before Saigon surrendered — bailed out the remaining Americans and rescued some 55,000 South Vietnamese in the last few weeks, but the debit side of the war is staggering.

Count the losses: fifty-five thousand Americans dead, another 300,000 wounded, thousands permanently disabled, the loss of 20 million good people to a brutal Communist regime. We spent $150 billion on this enterprise, all in vain. In the wake of this disaster, a new set of dominoes is now teetering on the brink: Laos, Thailand, South Korea, Burma, Indonesia, Portugal, Israel, etc.

To the last, despite all the Pollyanna talk about Hanoi desiring to negotiate, North Vietnam ruthlessly opted for the military subjugation of Saigon. On March 4, Hanoi began — in direct violation of the Paris Peace Accords — a massive offensive, committing all their reserve divisions in the north. South Vietnam, outgunned and outmanned, deprived of even fuel and ammunition because of the U.S. aid cutbacks, executed a hasty and disastrous retreat. It recouped to fight fiercely in such places as Xuan Loc, but it was beaten into submission. In the last days, as resistance collapsed, Hanoi, in effect, demanded unconditional surrender....

What is so terribly distressing about our defeat in Vietnam is that it need never have happened. While the liberals, with President Ford's approval, are so assiduously telling this country not to engage in recriminations, recriminations are clearly in order.

After suffering such a grave defeat, it is absolutely essential to discover what went wrong and

who took us there. How else are we to avoid such mistakes in the future? Whatever platitudes are being mouthed at the moment, the truth is the liberals do not want blame to be assessed precisely because of their overwhelming guilt in causing this catastrophe.

Certain things must not be allowed to pass into George Orwell's memory hole. The liberals took America into Vietnam. Then, after the majority of the sacrifices had been made and the job of saving South Vietnam was nearing completion, they deliberately and successfully worked to destroy any possibility that those sacrifices would be rewarded. That was their hideous crime, and it should not be casually forgotten.

BLAME MUST BE PLACED

The liberals who several years ago were urging us to cut and run and surrender in Vietnam are now strangely unwilling to discuss the question of who might be to blame. There is no need now to waste time trying to place the blame, they say. We must get on with the job.

Well, I disagree. This is exactly the time to place the blame and to find out who is responsible for the mess we have created in Indochina.

Senator Barry M. Goldwater, "Viet Blame Should Be Placed," **Human Events**, May 10, 1975, p. 19.

Under Presidents Kennedy and Johnson, the U.S. role in South Vietnam expanded until half-a-million American soldiers were in that country. Whatever other faults he may have had, President Nixon, through a masterful combination of diplomatic maneuvering and U.S. power, executed the withdrawal of those half-million men, got our prisoners of war released and still left South Vietnam standing, free from Communist control.

When the Paris Peace Accords were signed in January 1973, the President and Secretary of State Henry Kissinger were well aware that South Vietnam's survival still depended upon our capacity to threaten any new and massive Hanoi aggression with our B-52 bomber force in Thailand and our willingness to equip the South Vietnamese with the necessary weapons to resist something less than an all-out offensive. Yet after the peace accords were signed, the liberals then led a sustained drive to eliminate the very means at our disposal to prevent North Vietnam's conquest of South Vietnam.

There is no question but that Congress, dominated by the liberal Democrats, is to blame for this extraordinary defeat for the U.S., South Vietnam and the rest of the free world. When Sir Robert Thompson, the British military expert, commented to **Human Events** about the disaster unfolding in Indochina, he blamed the situation squarely on the U.S. lawmakers.

"First of all," he said, "they (Congress) stopped the bombing and made it impossible. They cut off the aid — so what did you expect to happen?" Maj. Gen. John Murray (U.S.A., Ret.), the senior officer representing the Defense Department from the time of the January 1973 cease-fire until mid-August 1974, was asked if there was a "direct relation" between the South Vietnamese Army's collapse and the congressional cut-off of aid. He responded: "There is no question whatever. It's an absolute relationship."...

Who were those who vigorously led the drive to scuttle South Vietnam's survival chances? Those names, despite media attempts to abjure finger pointing, should be recalled.

Sen. George McGovern (D.-S.D.), who has been serving Hanoi's constituency in the United States for the past several years, deserves high credit for undoing Saigon. Sen. Frank Church (D.-Idaho) played a distinguished role in betraying our Southeast Asian ally. Sen. Teddy Kennedy (D.-Mass.), Sen. Mike Mansfield (D.-Mont.), Sen. Thomas Eagleton (D.-Mo.), ex-Sen. J. W. Fulbright (D.-Ark.), Sen. Charles Percy (R.-Ill.) and Sen. Mark Hatfield (R.-Ore.) also served the anti-South Vietnam cause with vigor.

They were in the forefront of those to end, forever, any U.S. force in Indochina, even if the North Vietnamese, backed by the two Communist superpowers, Russia and China, massively violated the Paris accords.

As McGovern said when the Senate was passing the measure to prevent the Administration from renewing any bombing, a measure the Administration had repeatedly fought but accepted when it believed Congress would move up the bombing cut-off date. ''I could only feel a note of great satisfaction that, at long last, the Administration had finally capitulated on an issue some of us have been pressing in the Senate for a great many years.

''They finally agreed that a date certain would be acceptable to them and would be signed into law, so that as of August 15 (1973) — on or before August 15 — no more military involvement will take place anywhere in Indochina. Not only does that terminate the bombing in Cambodia and Laos, but also it forecloses the possibility of American military operations in North and South Vietnam.''

Having scrapped an essential tool to prevent North Vietnam from launching an all-out offensive, Congress began working to radically reduce the aid to South Vietnam.

Sir Robert Thompson believes that the most serious cutback came when the Senate approved on May 6, 1974, Teddy Kennedy's (D.-Mass.) amendment to a military supplemental aid bill to cut $266 million out of South Vietnam's defense budget. That aid cut, said Sir Robert, ''signified that perhaps the major lesson of the Vietnam War is: do not rely on the United States as an ally. This vote may prove to be one of the initial steps leading to the strategic surrender of the United States. May 6, 1974, may, therefore, become an important historical date.''

House members, of course, should also not be overlooked. Rep. Phillip Burton (D.-Calif.), Rep. Bella Abzug (D.-N.Y.) and Rep. Robert Carr (D.-Mich.) played important roles in causing South Vietnam's collapse. The South Vietnamese ambassador to the United States, Tram Kim Phuong, told **Human Events** a fortnight ago that President Thieu's decision to order what turned out to be a disastrous strategic retreat was based to a large extent on the March vote in the Democratic Caucus opposing further aid to South Vietnam, 189 to 49. Burton, who controls the Caucus, comprised of House Democratic members, encouraged the anti-South Vietnam vote, while both Abzug and Carr led the cut-off battle....

While others may have their own pet ideas as to why we suffered the cataclysmic defeat in Indochina, there can be no question that these liberal lawmakers deserve the major share of the credit. Political recriminations, in our view, are an idea whose time has long since come.

A FALSE CONCEPT
OF POWER

Charles A. Wells

Charles A. Wells is the editor and publisher of
Between The Lines, a semi-monthly newsletter of
liberal social and political opinion. Each issue
deals with major domestic and international
issues.

**Use the following questions to help your understanding
of the reading:**

1. What does Charles A. Wells mean by the phrase
   ''false concept of power?''
2. How does he describe the voices of hate and alarm?
3. How do you interpret the cartoon in this reading?
4. Why does the author say the South Vietnamese
   Army collapsed?

Excerpted from the May 1, and 15, 1975 issues of **Between The
Lines**. Reprinted with permission.

A false concept of power ends with the complete collapse of the U.S. political and military position in Southeast Asia — the false concept that through modern military technology the life of nations and movements of history could be controlled. Humanity cannot be controlled by armed might, we can only try to understand history and guide it. Or in some more rash moment — if the military retain their priorities — blow it all up....

Credibility and respect for our own Government is now going to be a problem for many American citizens. As the U.S. allies in Southeast Asia began to disintegrate, President Ford, Secretary of State Kissinger, Secretary of Defense Schlesinger and others all in turn put the blame on Congress and the ''indifference'' of the American people for the unspeakable tragedies occurring. This was on the face of it inaccurate, spiteful and childish, and they soon pulled themselves out of the first wave of hysteria and took postures more in keeping with the able, responsible gentlemen and leaders they really are.

Both President Ford and Secretary Kissinger however speak much of U.S. commitments in Southeast Asia. This is the crux of the matter, for the commitments were secret, made by the White House and Pentagon without consultation or consent of Congress or knowledge of the people. John F. Kennedy collaborated in plans to intervene in Vietnam with such hesitancy and anxiety (before assassination cut him down) that credit for escalation must fall on Lyndon Johnson and on Richard Nixon who doubled the cost in lives and money in three more years of warfare to ''get our boys home'' while continuing to ''meet our commitments.''

This subversion of the democratic practice and the usurpation of power finally aroused Congressional resistance and public disapproval, and Nixon's efforts at camouflage and compulsion led to Watergate: This is why the Ford and Kissinger efforts to enforce the adherence to ''commitments'' drag us back into the quagmire. Behind all the headlines and confusion, this is where the crisis really lies and on this issue much of our political and economic future hinges. For the exorbitant cost of war is now an arm of tyranny.

THE UNKNOWN SOLDIER

VIETNAM

LAST AMERICAN ASKED TO DIE FOR A MISTAKE

©1971 Chicago Daily News

Editorial cartoon by John Fischetti,
Courtesy of Field Newspaper Syndicate

There are forces in America that will not retreat from vindictiveness, who oppose all compromise and reconciliation. They think only in terms of armed might, though military power has proved to be a most cruel and costly delusion as a solution to political and economic problems. They would split the country and punish those who see a better world relationship through understanding and conciliation, labeling them as ''appeasers,'' falling back on the old terminologies and insanities of the cold war.

Since these voices of hate and alarm will be heard in every community, it is extremely important that as many citizens as possible be forearmed and informed, able to meet those who will accuse our country of the betrayal of our allies and of ourselves by not continuing war-like attitudes and actions.

The many accusations will include • that the failure to send more U.S. aid caused the defeat of the South Vietnamese armies (ARVN's); • that the loss of Hue and the Highlands was due to the lack of U.S. ammunition; • that STVN's failure was also caused by the lack of air support which we could have provided; • that

President Nguyen Van Thieu's leadership was undermined by lack of U.S. support as was the collapse of the Lon Nol regime in Cambodia; • that, in consequence all Southeast Asia and other areas will fall to the Reds "like dominoes" — a revival of the defense thesis prevalent during Korean war days; • that the collapse of the Kissinger Mideast negotiations was a consequence of the weakened U.S. position in Southeast Asia.

What Are The Facts?

Instead of the ARVN's lacking supplies, about $1 billion in U.S. military equipment and ammunition was abandoned to the North Vietnamese when ARVN units fled in disorder from Hue to the Highlands. (**N.Y. Times**, March 31; AP, April 1, etc.) Not unexpected since it has long been known that the Communists have, to an alarming degree, been supplied with U.S. arms sold and funneled to them by corrupt South Vietnamese. The enormous dimensions of this corruption is considerably due to the prodigious, wasteful outpouring of U.S. military supplies with scant supervision — as any U.S. veteran can testify. This goes to the heart of the matter, the misconception (and the military posture) that armed might means strength per se, when the opposite is true, unless controlled by economic and political wisdom and understanding.

Some Pentagon officials have fortunately spoken out and have told of the abundance of U.S. military supplies available to the ARVN forces and how neglect, irresponsibility, petty rivalries and lack of skills prevent the supplies from being used effectively. (The UPI and AP, March 31; **Newsweek** and **Time**, April 7.) More important, it has become known that the CIA and other intelligence agencies reported to the Pentagon recently that in their estimate the Communist nations supplied but $400 million in military aid to the North Vietnamese in '74, about a third of the $1.2 billion in aid the U.S. provided Saigon in that period. While the agencies added that their estimates might not be complete, it has always been conceded that three or four times more arms and firepower were used on the U.S.-ARVN side all through the war. Thus the amount of U.S. aid is not the real issue.

Air support inadequacies — or general lack of it —

doubtless hastened ARVN's disintegration. But the South Vietnamese had ample military planes available that were not used. Over 500 F-5E's and A-37's along with other bombers and fighters were known to be available. But poor maintenance, lack of reliable pilots, despite the training of thousands, kept most planes grounded. (Not a few planes are "lost," can't even be located.) On the other hand, the Communists did not introduce air power — no bombing or strafing. So ARVN can claim no imbalance. The Communists followed their usual strategy of massed artillery and rocket fire to blaze a murderous path through the countryside and cities as their armies advance. Latest reports tell of the North Vietnamese capturing most of ARVN's war planes, suddenly making Hanoi's Air Force the 7th largest in the world.

One reason few ARVN pilots were available is that the North Vietnamese are equipped with Russian quadruple mounted 23-mm anti-aircraft guns which the Arabs used so devastatingly against the Israeli squadrons of U.S. Phantoms in the October war of '73.

ARVN pilots have been notoriously unreliable in combat flying even when the U.S. Air Force rode their tails. They have, in the air as well as on the ground, *shown little heart for dying to save the Thieu regime and the landlords and rich traders that support him.*

The swathes of horribly destructive artillery and rocket fire with which the Communists sweep the way for their advance is of course a chief reason for the throngs of panicked refugees. To stay is to die. They have also been propagandized on the danger of a bloodbath. The Communists usually do execute those who have served as principal collaborators with opposing Governments, but it's selective killing and the bloodbath reports are nearly always exaggerated. Nonetheless, many innocent die — on both sides.

100,000 ARVN troops were around Hue and in the Highlands, doubtless more than the number of North Vietnamese since the latter are credited with having but 180,000 spread out over all South Vietnam — many even in the Delta below Saigon. So the ARVN were not outnumbered but were outmaneuvered, outfought, outgunned, because the ARVN had no discipline, no confidence in their commanders, knowing their generals were all corrupt. How can infantrymen be expected to stand and fight as Thieu ordered them to do when they see their officers flee with their wives and mistresses at the first salvo? The ARVN have little they can believe in, nothing to fight or die for. The major weapon the Communists have is a cause, something they can make men believe in. This lack of purpose of course undermined the U.S. presence in Vietnam, afflicting many GI's who had a sense of history and could see communism in perspective.

DIPLOMATIC SUICIDE

In other words our failure in Vietnam should force us to face seriously at last what is perhaps the most difficult proposition for Americans to accept: that even though much of the world admires our technology, envies our standard of living, or respects our might, the American model cannot be easily exported and is not relevant to huge parts of mankind. To see in other nations' efforts at shaping their own societies or a new international economic order a declaration of war on us would be both the apex of egocentrism and diplomatic suicide.

Stanley Hoffman, ''The Sulking Giant,'' **The New Republic**, May 3, 1975, p. 17.

As we've emphasized so often, communism is an evil, violent revolution that functions through tyranny. But when men become desperate for change and progress it can have appeal. The only way we can ''contain'' communism is to offer men a good revolution as an alternative to a bad revolution. None by heritage and resources are so equipped for that task as the American people....

Imprisonment and torture have been the lot of thousands of non-Communist Vietnamese under Thieu's rule, his prison system admittedly financed by U.S. dollars. (Again, the utter stupidity of thinking we could win with such a blind use of our aid and armed might.) The most sordid kinds of torture have been used continually, strategy in which the CIA participated from the beginning. The Phoenix program, set up by the CIA, to root out the Communist "infra-structure," was responsible for the torture and death of hundreds of innocent South Vietnamese. This project was organized by Wm. Colby, the present head of the CIA, a fact well publicized. Hence official Washington must share responsibility for the cruel and inhuman history of Thieu's regime.

RECOGNIZING ETHNOCENTRIC STATEMENTS

Instructions

Ethnocentrism is the tendency for people to feel their race, religion, culture, or nation is superior and to judge others by their own frame of reference. **Frame of reference** means the standards and values a person accepts because of his life experience and culture. A Marxist in Russia, for example, is likely to view things differently than a Christian in France.

Ethnocentrism has promoted much misunderstanding and conflict. It helps emphasize cultural differences and the notion that your nation's institutions are superior. Education, however, should stress the similarities of the human condition throughout the world and the basic equality and dignity of all men.

In order to avoid war and violence, people must realize how **ethnocentrism** and **frame of reference** limit their ability to be objective and understanding. Consider each of the following statements carefully. Mark **E** for any statement you think is ethnocentric. Mark **N** for any statement you think is not ethnocentric. Mark **U** if you are undecided about any statement.

E = Ethnocentric
N = Not Ethnocentric
U = Undecided

_____1. People of different cultures have many things in common.

_____2. God has marked the American people as his chosen nation.

_____3. Far more than rockets to the moon, Americans need solutions to their social and economic problems.

_____4. Nations of the world must develop the ability to cooperate.

_____5. We, the black people, are the original people of the planet earth.

_____6. Americans are not the chosen savior of mankind.

_____7. The Vietnamese people will have difficulty governing themselves in a civilized manner without the help of the U.S.

_____8. Many people have been helped by Communism.

_____9. In Brazil the urban terrorist movement has caused considerable concern.

_____10. The U.S. leads the world in doing the impossible, and history reflects no other national progress of such dimension and speed.

THE "NO-WIN" STRATEGY IN VIETNAM

M. Stanton Evans

M. Stanton Evans is a regular contributor to conservative journals of social and political opinion. He writes frequently in **Human Events**, and the **American Opinion** magazine, the latter a publication of the John Birch Society.

Use the following questions to assist you while reading:

1. Why does M. Stanton Evans say people are entitled to know who lost Vietnam?
2. Does the cartoon in this reading support any ideas expressed by the author?
3. According to the author, who is responsible for the "no win strategy" in Vietnam?

M. Stanton Evans, "Many Contributed to Vietnam Debacle," **Human Events**, May 24, 1975, p. 9. Reprinted with permission.

The disgrace in Indochina is now complete, and those who created it are painfully anxious to cover their tracks against political and historical judgment.

To this end, various commentators are busily arguing that there should be no recriminations about the twin disasters in Cambodia and Vietnam. It is crucial, we are told, to put the whole affair behind us. We should simply draw a veil across the bleeding corpse and go on about our business.

That people with much to answer for should take this attitude is understandable. All of us would prefer to tiptoe around our blunders and change the subject when we can. But the American people and the families of the American dead have quite a different interest in the matter. They are entitled to know who lost Vietnam, and why, to insure that this grotesque performance is not repeated.

Foremost on the list of those responsible for the confusion of American strategy in Vietnam are the functional agents of the opposition. It is incredible to reflect that while Americans were fighting and dying overseas our nation should have witnessed orgies of affection for the enemy, culminating more than once in massive marches and demonstrations guided by the agents of Hanoi. Much of this activity was aimed at sapping the national will to resist, and it emphatically is not to be forgotten.

These are also the gentry, by the way, who told us North Vietnam was not the aggressor in Indochina, that the war was simply a battle by indigenous guerrillas for a little social justice, and that fears of Communist expansion in the area were merest pipe dreams. Events of recent months have shown that these assurances, to put it mildly, were mistaken.

Coming next behind the explicit cheerleaders for Hanoi are members of Congress who decided at the crucial juncture to turn their backs on an endangered ally. These lawmakers would have us think Saigon went down because it lost "the will to fight." But the record suggests that had Congress provided the replacement parts and fuel so urgently needed by the anti-Communists, that will and the ability to implement it would have stayed intact. It was precisely the denial of necessary aid that precipitated the defeat.

In February, for example, when the Communist buildup was growing to ominous levels, half of South Vietnam's 1,200-craft air force was grounded for lack of parts. The remainder was subject to constraints on flying time through shortages of fuel. In the Mekong Delta, all combat helicopters were grounded. ARVN infantrymen were rationed to two grenades apiece instead of the former 10, and artillery fire was cut to one-third the rate prevailing at the time of the Paris accords. Those who produced this dismal outcome should be held accountable to history.

A MUD PUDDLE

If they'd handled (the Vietnam War) the way I wanted to handle it, Henry Kissinger wouldn't have to be traveling. I could have ended it in a month. I would have made North Vietnam look like a mud puddle.

Senator Barry M. Goldwater quoted in the **National Observer** and reprinted in the **Minneapolis Tribune**, November 11, 1972, p. 6A.

Also to be remembered, in slightly different context, are those who got us into this war in the first place, on a basis that made it impossible to win. These were the liberal strategists of limited warfare and gradual buildup who flourished in the Kennedy-Johnson years, and who evolved our fuzzy halfway commitment to Vietnam. Their notion was to fight a static, defensive struggle, leaving the initiative to the enemy — a perfect formula for perpetual involvement.

Compounding this original ''no-win'' strategy was the liberal-prompted overthrow of President Ngo Dinh Diem, in obedience to our usual notions of reforming other nations in our own political image. The war from that point forward began to deteriorate, and American troops were thrown in to fill the resulting vacuum. It was this commitment of U.S. ground forces, long opposed by military thinkers, that proved to be the psychological crusher for America.

Finally, we must not omit the strategists of detente. These include the Democratic authors of our involvement in Vietnam and their Republican successors headed by Henry Kissinger. Under this peculiar doctrine — still enshrined in Washington — we were supposed to fight the Communists in Vietnam while supplying equipment and technology to their masters in the Kremlin. Thus the grim anomaly of American planes bombarding Soviet trucks, while American companies built for Moscow the largest truck factory in the world.

WIELDING THE BIG STICK

LACK OF NATIONAL RESOLVE

U.S. FOREIGN POLICY

Distributed by L.A. Times Syndicate

Editorial cartoon by Don Hesse
Copyright, **St. Louis Globe Democrat**
Reprinted with permission of Los Angeles Times Syndicate

And thus as well the supreme confusion of the American people, instructed by their diplomatic leaders to battle communism at the regional level while embracing it at the global level. The proposition was ridiculous on the face of it, and U.S. citizens increasingly came to see it in that light. If communism is something we can cheerfully live with in Peking and Moscow, why should we keep spending billions to prevent its triumph in Saigon?

(The bankruptcy of detente-as-usual was well exemplified by President Ford in his climactic address requesting aid to South Vietnam. The President urged the Congress to stand by our commitments to an anti-Communist ally, and asserted that detente was not a license to fish in troubled waters. He then concluded with the proposal that Congress grant most-favored-nation status to the Soviet Union.)

Detente also played a specific role in the meaningless peace accord negotiated by Kissinger with so much fanfare. This empty compact left the Communists in place in South Vietnam and provided no effective machinery for preventing further warfare. Yet Kissinger blandly promoted it as peace-with-honor, in keeping with his grand design of global concord with the enemy. Where, one wonders, is peace with honor now?

There are others, of course, who contributed to the debacle, but these will do for starters. If we are to avoid a repetition of this horror, the people and concepts responsible for it should be fully understood. Recriminations are therefore very much in order, and we should waste no time in getting to them.

READING **12**

A GENERATION
OF DECEIT

The Progressive

> **The Progressive** is a liberal journal of social and political opinion. National and international problems and issues are dealt with each week by the editors; and numerous articles and editorials by other liberal spokesmen appear regularly.

Use the following questions to help your understanding of the reading:

1. Who do the editors of **The Progressive** say betrayed America in Vietnam?
2. Why do they say the American intervention was no mistake? What was it?
3. According to the editors, what kind of people in foreign countries place the imperial interests of the U.S. above the welfare of their own people?
4. How do you interpret the cartoon in this reading?

"A Generation of Deceit," **The Progressive**, June, 1975, pp. 5, 6. Reprinted by permission from **The Progressive**, 408 West Gorham Street, Madison, Wisconsin 53703. Copyright © 1975, The Progressive, Inc.

The post-mortem examinations of the Great Indochina Debacle are under way, and some of them almost rival the war itself as exercises in criminal stupidity. We have heard, in recent weeks, dark mutterings from President Ford, Vice President Rockefeller, and Secretary of State Kissinger that Congress "gave away" South Vietnam and Cambodia by refusing at long last to pour any more American treasure into the bottomless pit of "military aid." We have seen suggestions that the Stars and Stripes would still be flying in Saigon if Nguyen Van Thieu had not lost his will — or if Richard M. Nixon had not lost his marbles. (Columnist William F. Buckley: "What would Nixon, under Kissinger's prodding, have done, if his reactions had been healthy, when only a few weeks after the Paris accord was executed, the North began its blatant disregard of it? My own information is that it was planned, some time in April, to pulverize Hanoi and Haiphong. If that had been done, not only would the North Vietnamese juggernaut have disintegrated, an entirely new meaning would have attached to the concept of detente.")

After twenty-five agonizing years — it was on May 8, 1950, that the Truman Administration decided to help the French in their Indochina war — American politicians and pundits persist in their attempts to deceive themselves, and the rest of us, about the causes and consequences of this nation's intervention. After the loss of 50,000 American (and no one knows how many Asian) lives, after the squandering of $150 billion, after the destruction of several hapless countries and the disruption of our own, we are still offered the same lame explanations, excuses, rationalizations, lies.

As Washington's Cambodian clients fled Phnom Penh to join their bank accounts in the West, President Ford was moved to express his "admiration" for them — a touching sentiment, as Anthony Lewis observed in **The New York Times**, "for politicians who fattened on American aid as their people starved; for military officers who made their soldiers pay for the rice sent by the United States — or supplied no food, so that some were reduced to cannibalism; for officials who forced United Nations relief agencies to pay $100,000 for the privilege of flying in powdered milk for starving Cambodian children."

Roy Justus in **The Minneapolis Star**

As the American-created government in Saigon crumbled, Secretary Kissinger warned: ''We shall not forget who supplied the arms which North Vietnam used to make a mockery of its signature on the Paris accords.'' Is there anyone left who does not understand that American arms in Vietnam have far exceeded those on ''the other side,'' or that the United States and its Vietnamese puppets have made a mockery of every attempt at a negotiated settlement at least since the Geneva accords of 1954?

If we understand nothing else after this calamitous quarter of a century, let us understand this: America was not "betrayed" in Indochina — not by its enemies, not by its allies, not by those of its own citizens who mounted heroic resistance against a criminal war. The *denouement* that we have witnessed in the last few weeks was the logical and inevitable consequence of American policy and practice, and it was clear, at least to some of us, almost from the beginning....

And if we understand nothing else, let us understand this: The American intervention in Indochina was not a "mistake," not a "miscalculation," not a "blunder." It was a conscious and consistent series of decisions deliberately taken in furtherance of a grand design for creation of American Empire — in Asia and wherever else the United States could get away with it. The dreamers of that dream, the architects of that design began their work decades ago; their roster encompasses Dean Acheson and Harry Truman no less than Kissinger and Nixon, and it includes the Bundys and Rostows and Dulleses and their "bipartisan" allies in Congress who sold Americans on the fatuous notion that "politics stops at the water's edge."

They knew that most Americans dreamed a different dream — of democracy and justice and peace — and so they did their best to disguise their sundry adventures. As we now know from official records, they mounted secret wars and financed furtive coups. They invented "incidents" (as in the Gulf of Tonkin) and "enemies" (as in Chile) and "threats" (as in Cuba). They concocted a whole new language to conceal the grim realities of the atrocities being committed in our names: "protective reaction," "interdiction," "defoliation," "targetting."And everywhere in the world, as in Indochina, they made common cause with the greedy, the corrupt, and the despotic — for, after all, who else was available as an "ally" who would place the imperial interests of the United States above those of his own people?

It is finished, in Indochina, but we are not finished with the world. Secretary of State Kissinger, in one of his pathetic last-minute appeals to Congress to pour another few hundred million dollars down the rathole of Vietnam, spoke of his determination "to avoid the impression that the United States is not capable of mastering events." The dream of empire is hard dying.

AMERICA'S SCORE FAR HIGHER

In terms of the number of lives taken and of lands laid waste, America's score is, unhappily, far higher than any other country's since the end of World War II.

Would I rather be a Vietnamese who was being "saved" by the American army, or be a Czech who was being "saved" by the Russian army?

Of course, I would rather be the Czech. The number of lives taken and the amount of devastation caused by the 1968 Russian military intervention in Czechoslovakia were small, measured by the standard of America's record in Vietnam.

Arnold J. Toynbee, "U.S. Seen As Most Dangerous Country," New York Times Service. (Reprinted in the **Minneapolis Tribune**, May 5, 1970.)

Kissinger is hardly the sole custodian of that dream. While we second the motion that it is time for the Secretary of State to resign and devote his time to serene contemplation of his Nobel Peace Prize, we harbor no illusion that his departure would, of itself, solve any of our problems — any more than did the departure of Acheson or Dulles or Dean Rusk.

The durable dream of empire was manifest in the President's foreign policy address to Congress on April 11, in which he trotted out again the weary old phrases of American hegemony: "The leadership of the United States....the luxury of abdication or domestic discord....sensationalized public debate over legitimate intelligence activities....we cannot afford indecision, disunity, or disarray....the world looks to us for vigor and vision."

The world looks to us — to the extent that it looks to us at all — for a return to the traditional American ideals and values. It looks to us for recognition, however belatedly, that other peoples share the goals we enunciated 200 years ago — independence, life, liberty, and the pursuit of happiness. It looks to us for acceptance of the historic fact that the era of empires has ended.

The world looks to us for a sign that we have learned something from the experience of Indochina so that we will not repeat the exercise again next week, next month, next year in Italy or Portugal or Latin America or the Middle East.

It was said of the Bourbons of France that they remembered everything and learned nothing. After a generation of deceit, it is time for us to level with the world and ourselves.

DISTINGUISHING BIAS FROM REASON

One of the most important critical thinking skills is the ability to distinguish between opinions based on emotions or bias and conclusions based on a rational consideration of facts. This discussion exercise is designed to promote experimentation with one's capacity to recognize biased statements.

Some of the following statements have been taken from the readings in this chapter and some have other origins. Consider each statement carefully. Mark **R** for any statement you feel is based on a rational consideration of the facts. Mark **P** for any statement you believe is based on prejudice or emotion. Mark **I** for any statement you think is impossible to judge. Then discuss and compare your judgments with other class members.

R = REASON
P = PREJUDICE
I = IMPOSSIBLE TO JUDGE

_____1. The CIA and other intelligence agencies reported that in their estimate the Communist nations supplied but $400 million in military aid to the North Vietnamese in 1974, about a third of the $1.2 billion in aid the U.S. provided Saigon in that period.

_____2. There is no question but that Congress, dominated by the liberal Democrats, is to blame for this extraordinary defeat for the U.S. in South Vietnam.

_____3. Chicanos are fair with each other but ruthless in their dealings with others.

_____4. Indians are as friendly as other people.

_____5. Jews have money and power out of all proportion to their numbers.

_____6. Jews are behind the communist menace in the U.S.

_____7. Jews are similar in behavior to other people.

_____8. Italians usually try to exert control and influence over others.

_____9. White people will more than likely succeed in education.

_____10. The Chinese Americans will always remain a foreign and alien element.

_____11. The Irish in America are proud of their heritage and tradition.

_____12. White people discriminate against others.

_____13. Most black people fail to keep up their personal appearances and neighborhoods.

_____14. Many Mexican Americans live in the Southwestern part of the U.S.

_____15. Most Germans are patriotic individuals.

_____16. Most Mexican Americans are friendly and sociable.

CHAPTER **3**

LESSONS AND CONSEQUENCES

COMMUNIST BLOODBATH LIKELY IN POST-WAR INDOCHINA

John Ashbrook

John Ashbrook is a Republican representative from Ohio. His political writings frequently appear in conservative publications. The following remarks are excerpted from his recent study on Communist atrocities.

Consider the following questions while reading:

1. According to John Ashbrook, what must the liberal press not be allowed to forget?
2. Why does he fear a bloodbath in a Communist controlled Vietnam? What evidence does he offer to support his contention?
3. Can you relate the cartoon in this reading to any ideas expressed by John Ashbrook?

John Ashbrook, "Why Asian Refugees Won't Go Back," **Human Events**, May 17, 1975, p. 5. Reprinted with permission.

The present tragic events now unfolding in Cambodia and South Vietnam raise ominous signs once again of the prospects of a Communist-style bloodbath in Southeast Asia. It is urgent that the on-going controversy over the fact or fiction of bloodbaths not be allowed to place in jeopardy the lives of those marked for extinction by the North Vietnamese, the Vietcong, and the Khmer Rouge.

The liberal press and those apologists who blindly belittle the possibility of large-scale reprisals against the South Vietnamese and Cambodians, whose only crime was their quest for freedom, must not be permitted to forget the mass slaughter at Hue or Dak Son or the estimated 36,000 civilians killed by Communist terrorists between 1957 and 1971. Those are recent history. The liberal, of course, sneers that the Stalinist purges or even the Chinese mass executions of the early '50s is no longer their policy.

Unclassified telegrams from our embassy in Saigon in the last several months have described the brutal, cold-blooded killing of innocent South Vietnamese civilians, law enforcement personnel, South Vietnamese government officials and employees and captured South Vietnamese soldiers, as told by refugees from the occupied areas. As the United States lost over 50,000 American lives in Vietnam helping to defend South Vietnam against such Communist violence and terror, I am introducing legislation to establish a select House Committee to investigate and report to the House all accounts of executions, abductions, willful woundings and other denials of basic human rights in Southeast Asia by all Communist forces against civilians, military, police and government personnel.

A recent State Department telegram from Saigon describes the killing of about 300 South Vietnamese government employees and police, as related by an eye-witness to a Saigon police captain. Families of the victims were led out of town by several guards and explosions in their midst, presumably mortars, killed some and wounded others before the panicked crowd ran into the woods.

Another telegram dispatched from the U.S. Mission in Saigon recently read:

PERIOD OF
ADJUSTMENT

Editorial cartoon by Don Hesse
Copyright, **St. Louis Globe Democrat**
Reprinted with permission of Los Angeles Times Syndicate

''According to refugees that had witnessed several executions carried out by VC local forces and infrastructure, on outskirts of Danang GVN policemen were beheaded and groups of soldiers tied together and killed with grenades. Based on their observations, refugees said that it appeared that VC local forces were systematically liquidating GVN security personnel. They added that regular NVA forces did not appear to be participating in the executions.''

State Department telegram No. 2492 reads in part:

''We have received report from GVN official who

had interviewed number National police escapees from MR-1 that Communists have systematically searched out both national police and special branch personnel and in most cases executed these personnel as soon as they were discovered. He cited example of district police official in MR-1 who was hiding near his home.... When his mother complained that her son had done nothing to deserve execution, mother was executed by Communist soldier who fired single pistol shot into her head."

Another recent State Department telegram alleges further brutalities:

"The monks in a Ban Me Thuot pagoda were accused of helping people hide from the 'PRG' (they had in fact sheltered and fed a number of escaped) and were led to the marketplace in Ban Me Thuot, the day after the fighting stopped. Several thousand other people were also assembled there. All were told to sit down."

The telegram continues:

"Then local 'PRG' cadre walked through the crowd, pointing out GVN (Government of Viet Nam) employees and police known to them. About 300, according to the monk, were selected and taken off to one side. The presiding cadre delivered a lengthy harangue, accusing them of being American lackeys and spies, and enemies of the people. They were all shot and killed."

In his letter of April 18, 1975, to selected members of Congress, President George Meany of the AFL-CIO provided still other accounts of Communist barbarism. The information, received by phone from Saigon on April 18, 1975, is a rough account from the CVT, South Vietnam's confederation of labor. Mr. Meany noted that —

"As in the case of every other Communist takeover in every other country, the free trade union movement is an early and specially targeted victim."

The cases cited by the CVT are as follows:

"In Quang Tin, they rounded up all of the police force. Some were shot out of hand. With others, they drove nails through their heels, wired them together and led them off to the jungle. That was the last seen of them. Some of the military were also treated in the same way.

"In Danang, CVT officers were arrested, required to turn over all of their records. The CVT members of the transportation workers (Lambretta drivers, etc.) were pressed into driving supplies to the front. This report was received from a CVT man who escaped and was barely coherent.

"At Ban Me Thuot, one of the CVT people escaped from there. The population of the town was assembled and divided into different categories. All of the leading citizens were taken away and have not been seen since. The males between 16 and 22 were drafted into the military forces and sent directly into combat. Each family was redesignated and put into a peoples' union to mobilize a labor force and were subject to 'people's justice.' The former union officials were put on a non-subsistence ration.

"In Binh Long, the plantation workers' representative was shot and others were arrested."

On Saturday, April 19, the Washington **Post** ran a front-page treatment of the current controversy over whether a bloodbath will ensue in South Vietnam if the North Vietnamese and the Vietcong take over all of Vietnam. The **Post** items, actually two separate articles, was headlined: "Bloodbath, A Theory Becomes a Fear."

One excerpt from the article by Michael Getler and Marilyn Berger reads:

"And, if historical patterns are a guide, many officials believe it will take many more months for an actual 'bloodbath' in the south to unfold if it is going to happen."

Well, I have news for the officials mentioned above — it has happened in South Vietnam, starting back in 1957.

In its very useful compendium, "The Human Cost of

Communism in Vietnam," issued by the Senate Internal Security subcommittee in 1972, the total civilian victims of Communist terror in South Vietnam from 1957 through November 1971 amounted to 36,181 killed and 53,758 abducted. This did not include the estimated 10,000 civilians who lost their lives during the 1968 Tet offensive or the more than 3,000 civilians disinterred from the graves at Hue, or the estimated 2,000 killed during the second phase of the Hue massacre.

KINDLY "UNCLE HO"

Historians estimate that kindly "Uncle Ho," by 1947, had physically eliminated all his political rivals including powerful Vietnamese Trotskyite leaders. During a two-month period in the Fall of 1945, some 10,000 persons were "eliminated" in Hanoi alone.

"North Vietnam's Long War of Planned Atrocities," **The Mindszenty Report**, September, 1972, p. 1.

While some may argue over the semantics of the term "Bloodbath" — how many does one have to murder and in what period of time? — the sad case of Hue certainly qualifies. Some bodies were mutilated and others were found in conditions indicating that death had been caused by being buried alive.

Among those found were Mr. Tran Dien, a senator in South Vietnam's National Assembly, four officials of the Vietnam Nationalist party, hamlet chiefs and their wives, teachers, shopkeepers, students, and children. The victims also included two French priests and three German doctors from the Hue University Medical School.

Survivors told of the Vietcong's summary trials, torture and condemnation of civilians — including women and schoolboys — on such charges as being a "reactionary" or "opposing the revolution."

A father of nine was buried alive because he had a son in the South Vietnamese Army. Some were forced to dig their own graves, and many who were called by Vietcong agents to attend a political education meeting were never seen again by their families. A Buddhist monk at the Tang Quang Tu Pagoda reported over-hearing Vietcong execution parties working each night during the first two weeks of February 1968.

Although the massacre at Dak Son did not approach the magnitude of the Hue bloodbath, pictures of Dak Son babies killed at pointblank range by flamethrowers — such pictures were in the past available for the asking from the Defense Department — convey the unbelievable depravity of Communist terror.

Dak Son, a hamlet of 2,000 Montagnard people consisting of mostly unarmed women and children and defended by a small militia, was attacked by the Vietcong with machinegun, mortar, and rocket fire — and 60 flamethrowers. The militiamen were surrounded and isolated, and for the rest of the night ignored by the marauders.

The Vietcong were not intent on a military victory but on a cold-blooded, monumental massacre of the Dak Son inhabitants. Houses and inhabitants were set afire by the Vietcong along with everything in sight: trees, fences, gardens, chickens, grain from the annual harvest. Structures that withstood the fiery attack were leveled by grenades.

RECONCILIATION, NOT BLOODLETTING, WILL BE COMMUNIST POLICY

Don Luce

Don Luce is Director of Clergy and Laymen Concerned (CALC). In 1967 he resigned as Director of International Voluntary Services in South Viet Nam and wrote, with 48 colleagues, a letter to President Lyndon Johnson calling for an end to bombing, defoliation and forced refugee movement, and for the beginning of negotiations and recognition of the NLF. He was kicked out of South Viet Nam in 1971 after exposing the tiger cages on Con So Island where political prisoners and opponents of the Saigon regime were held under inhumane conditions.

As you read try to answer the following questions:

1. Why does Don Luce think Communist leaders in South Vietnam will pursue a policy of reconciliation?
2. What people does he say will lose the most as a result of the Communist victory in Vietnam?
3. Who does he say will benefit the most from this victory?
4. How do you interpret the cartoon in this reading?

Don Luce, ''Vietnam: Opening the Gates,'' **Christianity and Crisis**, May 26, 1975, pp. 122, 23. Reprinted from the May 26, 1975 issue of **Christianity and Crisis**. Copyright © 1975 by **Christianity and Crisis**.

Reconciliation, not bloodbath, will be the most likely policy of the Revolutionary Government of the Republic of South Viet Nam for three reasons: (1) The most corrupt people and those who directed the interrogations and torture have left the country. (2) Reconciliation, not bitterness, is necessary for rebuilding the country; for example, such a policy is the best way to get the doctors, engineers and agriculturalists who are in France and the US back to Viet Nam. (3) The people are tired of the killing.

The Vietnamese are extremely proud of their culture, which dates back thousands of years. By inviting Quaker and Mennonite volunteers to remain in the liberated areas, the new authorities have already demonstrated a willingness to let the world know what is going on there. The international press, including journalists from CBS and Associated Press, are already reporting from Da Nang and other South Vietnamese cities.

This is not to say that no one will be worse off or suffer from the change in government. Life will be hard for the privileged class that remained behind. A redistribution of income necessarily means that some people have a lot to lose. Everyone will be expected to do his/her share in the country's reconstruction. Doctors will receive no more than dock workers; contractors who made their living through manipulating American aid will become laborers. For families who have enjoyed servants, chauffeured automobiles and lavish cocktail parties, this will be a difficult adjustment.

The people who will lose most from the Saigon Government's demise are those who profited the most from the war. These people — military officers, contractors, interrogators and corrupt Saigon officials — lived luxuriously by associating closely with the US effort.

Many left on the refugee flights for Guam and the US. Life will not be easy in a different culture. While Americans approved of the refugee lift, no big brass bands have welcomed the new citizens to our shores. Many resent the fact that Vietnamese will now compete with unemployed Americans for scarce jobs.

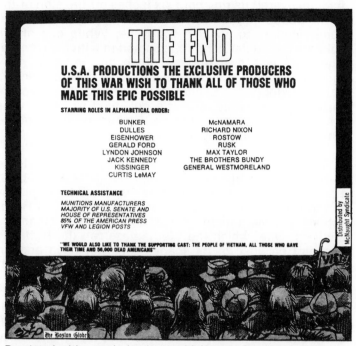

Reprinted with permission by the McNaught Syndicate, Inc.

Who will benefit? More than 10 million South Vietnamese farmers were moved into the cities in the sixties and early seventies in an attempt to deprive the liberation forces of food, soldiers and intelligence information. These people have the most to gain from the war's end: They can go back to their farms! For the majority of Vietnamese peace means a time to celebrate and a time of hard work.

However, the joyous return to the rice fields will be filled with danger. Farmers will find their land filled with mines and pock-marked with bomb craters. In 1973 I visited a village in the liberated area of Quang Tri province. ''Don't leave the paths and plowed fields,'' I was told. ''There are a lot of mines out there. Most of our buffalo have been killed and even some of the children. It's very dangerous.''

I thought the warnings were to impress the foreigner rather than a reflection of any real danger. After all, people had been farming the fields for over a year. But on the second day, as we walked along a path, someone shouted: ''Hey, there's a mine!'' The typhoon rains had uncovered its tip about six inches off the side of the path. The children with us went running back to get some soldiers to unearth the mine. While one of the soldiers began defusing it, I zoomed in with my camera. The man was sweating — obviously nervous. As I moved closer to record a bead of perspiration on his chin, he stopped. "Excuse me," he said. "But you're making me nervous, and it's not good to be nervous when you're defusing a mine." I hurried away as he finished disconnecting the wires.

Experience from World War II indicates that the mine-clearing will take 25 years. Another task will be to find the antipersonnel bomblets dispersed by airplanes in the rural areas thought to contain Provisional Revolutionary Government (PRG) and North Vietnamese soldiers. One, which the Vietnamese call the Butterfly bomblet because of its shape, does not have enough explosive power to kill a person, but it does shear off the bottom part of the leg.

A generation of youth must be trained in rice agriculture. Many children were moved to the cities at an early age. They are now in their late teens and early twenties and have no farm experience. Normally the young learn to farm at the side of their parents. The experiences of shining shoes, pimping and pushing drugs in the cities are of no value now.

Billions of dollars worth of American equipment was left behind — airports, planes, seaports and four-lane highways. Da Nang airport was once the busiest in the world. Cam Ranh port is one of the world's best natural harbors. To the average person the scrap metal will be a great resource. Steel from abandoned tanks is being pounded into plowshares. The multicolored, plastic-covered copper wiring from former US communications systems is being woven into baskets and handbags. Discarded ammunition crates have been used to build hospitals, schools and homes.

Orphans will also benefit from the change in government. There are no orphanages in the PRG area because children were adopted by relatives or neighbors and provided for within the extended family structure. In contrast to the PRG the Thieu Government discouraged adoptions by restrictive laws. For example, to adopt a child a couple had to have been married 10 years and have no natural children of their own *or* get permission from the President.

AMERICAN PRESENCE CORRUPTED VIETNAMESE

The American presence of soldiers, arms, and money poisoned and corrupted Vietnamese society. American bombing all but destroyed the country. The regimes in the South, that were created and nurtured by American power, had corruption and repression as their basic characteristics. The rulers of the American client regimes got rich while their people were hungry and homeless. They imprisoned and tortured their own people for dissent or even neutrality, and kept demanding ever more money and weapons from their American benefactors. They were regimes created by the American war in Indochina and they needed war to sustain themselves.

Jim Wallis, "Vietnam and Repentance," **Post American**, May, 1975, p. 20.

Political prisoners have been released. As provincial and district capitals in central Viet Nam changed administrations, the prisoners were freed and literally tore down the prison walls.

The new government. We can expect the new government officials in South Viet Nam to have an honest and simple life style. The new province and district chiefs will come from the farm population and behave differently from the colonels previously put in power by Saigon. There will be no more flamboyant Marshall Nguyen Cao Ky's!

US-Viet Nam relations. Viet Nam will be united. The two regions are complementary — the north has industry and minerals, the south rich agricultural land. More important the Vietnamese see themselves as one people. A unified Viet Nam will not be run by one section of the country any more than one region can dictate policies here.

The Vietnamese policy toward America will be to establish diplomatic ties as soon as possible. Even during the war the North Vietnamese tried to keep channels of communication open with the American people so that with peace friendly relations can be established.

Journalists who visited North Viet Nam during the war included Walter Cronkite, Pulitzer Prize winners Peter Arnett and Frances Fitzgerald, and **Newsweek's** Senior Editor Arnold De Borschgrave. Doctors, lawyers and religious leaders have traveled through North Viet Nam. Even Henry Kissinger was in Hanoi in 1973! In December, when Prime Minister Pham Van Dong met him with a group of US religious leaders — including the Roman Catholic Bishop of Gary, Indiana and the Methodist Bishop of Chicago — he told them how much he appreciated their visit. It would be nice, he said, if North Vietnamese religious leaders could return the visit.

I found no animosity toward Americans during my visits to North Viet Nam and the PRG areas of South Viet Nam. "The kings in our history who built great walls always lost," claims Hoang Hung, the director of the historical museum in Hanoi. "The ones who opened their gates won. We want to open our gates to many Americans — teachers, religious leaders, students. We think understanding is very precious. We should not be afraid of each other."

It will not take 25 years to play a game of ping-pong with the Vietnamese!

DISTINGUISHING FACT FROM OPINION

This discussion exercise is designed to promote experimentation with one's ability to distinguish between fact and opinion. It is a fact, for example, that the United States was militarily involved in the Vietnam War. But to say this involvement served the interests of world peace is an opinion or conclusion. Future historians will agree that American soldiers fought in Vietnam, but their interpretations about the causes and consequences of the war will probably vary greatly.

Some of the following statements are taken from readings in this chapter and some have other origins. Consider each statement carefully. Mark **O** for any statement you feel is an opinion or interpretation of the facts. Mark **F** for any statement you believe is fact. Then discuss and compare your judgments with those of other class members.

O = OPINION
F = FACT

_____1. Reconciliation, not bloodbath, will be the most likely policy of the revolutionary government of the Republic of South Vietnam.

_____ 2. The communist government will engineer a bloodbath in South Vietnam.

_____ 3. The Vietcong won a military victory in South Vietnam.

_____ 4. The Saigon government of President Thieu was corrupt.

_____ 5. In no instance was communist aggression more evident than in Hanoi's military intervention in South Vietnam.

_____ 6. Since President Ford pardoned Richard Nixon, he should grant unconditional amnesty to the draft resistors.

_____ 7. Americans, not just the communists, shot civilians, tortured prisoners, bombed hospitals, napalmed children and gave medals to those who did so.

_____ 8. Through violence and aggression, communist forces took control of South Vietnam.

_____ 9. The U.S. cannot act as the policeman of the world.

_____ 10. All communists in the U.S. are traitors.

_____ 11. American military forces still remain in Thailand.

_____ 12. From our Vietnam experience, Americans should learn that it does not pay to appease the communists.

_____ 13. Americans committed war crimes in Vietnam if the standards by which we executed Nazi leaders after World War II were applied to us (as we announced at Nuremberg they should be).

_____ 14. For America the Indochina war was costly and divisive.

APPEASEMENT OF COMMUNISTS MUST END

Morrie Ryskind

Morrie Ryskind is a conservative political commentator. His articles appear frequently in **Human Events** and **The Manchester Union Leader**. They also are carried by the **Washington Star Syndicate**.

Think of the following questions while you read:

1. According to Morrie Ryskind, what is the great lesson of Vietnam?
2. Does the cartoon in this reading support the author's ideas?
3. What does the author say about the liberal attitude?

Morrie Ryskind, ''Communist Pledges Written on the Wind,'' **Human Events**, May 24, 1975, pp. 11, 12. © 1975 **Washington Star Syndicate**. Reprinted by permission.

The liberal media are up to their navels in editorials that solemnly proclaim there is a great lesson for all of us in Saigon. Indeed there is, but the lesson is not new and should have been learned long ago: that Communist pledges are written on wind and in water and are completely untrustworthy. Fifty years of unabated Communist perfidy testify that this postulate has withstood every test and warrants being ranked as an axiom as sound as any of Euclid's.

There was Stalin, who tried and executed thousands of old Bolsheviks for "collaborating with fascists"; there were his pacts of friendship with Estonia, Latvia and Lithuania, after which those nations were "incorporated" into the USSR; his invasion of Finland, Hungary and Poland; the infamous Katyn Massacre, which he blamed on the Germans, but which proved to be planned and carried out under his orders. And, post Stalin, the seizure of Czechoslovakia.

THE DOMINOES ARE FALLING

During the past several years it has been popular to ridicule the "Domino Theory." Tragic events are now testifying to its truth. The dominoes that have already fallen are Cambodia, South Vietnam, and Laos, while Thailand is shaking. Every country in Southeast Asia is feeling the shock and the major question seems to be the order in which they will fall.

Fred Schwarz, **Christian Anti-Communism Crusade**, June 15, 1975, p. 4.

And under Mao, millions of "rightwing deviationists" were murdered, with the rivers running red with their blood; while Ho, if not in the same league with the two Red champs, managed to kill a goodly number of farmers, teachers, lawyers, doctors and civil servants who represented Saigon's best.

To be fair, most of these atrocities made our liberals recoil — for a week or so. But after that,

they returned to normalcy and, if conservatives referred to these crimes, we were accused of trying to revive the Cold War and called "Red baiters."

But in no instance was communism's naked aggression more clearly evident than in Hanoi's resumption of the Vietnamese war, despite the pace under which not only Hanoi but Russia and China pledged to both Saigon and America that they would adhere to the agreement that brought Le Duc Tho the Nobel Peace Prize.

Yet — as I've noticed before and intend to keep on noting — this time no rebuke has come from the liberal media. Maybe, as Pope said of vice, they first endured, then pitied, and now embrace the monster. They even tend to accept the Orwellian Newspeak in which the Reds cloak the fact that they are the rapists, not the rapees. The art of semantics can cover an enormity of sins.

Thus, as we learned during the Hollywood Academy Awards, the Reds "liberated" Saigon. And we have "forcibly evacuated" some 100,000 Saigonese, with another 100,000 fleeing from their liberators in any sort of boat, vehicle, cart or, in extremis, even shanks' mare — just as many of these same folk originally fled from the People's Paradise of Hanoi to the "corrupt" southern sector — Saigon.

The liberal attitude is epitomized by the two "victory parades" at Berkeley, Calif., the recognized center of university avant-garde thinking. There the elite made no pretense of being anti-war (as was alleged in earlier demonstrations) but hailed the rout of America, waved Hanoi's flag, and chanted praise of Ho Chi Minh. There is even some talk of changing the name of a campus street to Ho Chi Minh Road. (Though I think Murderer's Row would be more apt.)

I don't know where these youngsters learned their history, but when they can cheer for Ho, I feel something is wrong. Don't they know that when his forces first took Hue, Ho had 3,500 civilians shot and buried them in unmarked graves?

MR. POLITICIAN

Political comic strip by Ranan Lurie
Copyright, **Los Angeles Times**
Reprinted with permission

I fear I'm out of step, for having been raised on Dick Merriwell and Horatio Alger, I root for the good guys against the bad. So I doff my hat to Ambassador Graham Martin, who hoped to save Saigon and was the last American official to leave it. When a liberal reporter argued Martin should have left earlier, Kissinger retorted, "He was loyal to the people whom he had served, hardly the worst of faults."

And I likewise salute Rep. Thomas Morgan (D.-Pa.) for a gallant attempt to have the House vote $327 million in emergency funds for the Saigon refugees. The Senate had okayed the measure, but the more liberal House defeated it, 246 to 162. Any time they want to change the name of my own street to Thomas Morgan Road, I'll go along gladly.

U.S. CANNOT ACT AS THE WORLD'S POLICEMAN

Robert McAfee Brown

Robert McAfee Brown was a Navy chaplain in World War II and is now Professor of Religious Studies at Stanford University. He was active in both the Civil Rights Movement and the Anti-War Movement.

Consider the following questions while reading:

1. Why does Robert McAfee Brown say that to forget Vietnam would be a disaster?
2. What things does he say we should learn from Vietnam?
3. How do you interpret the cartoon in this reading?

Robert McAfee Brown, ''On Forgetting Viet Nam,'' **Christianity and Crisis**, May 23, 1975, pp. 154, 55. Reprinted from the May 23, 1975 issue of **Christianity and Crisis**. Copyright © 1975 by **Christianity and Crisis**.

President Ford is urging us "to put Viet Nam behind us," to avoid recriminations, to look to the future instead of the past; in short, to "forget" Viet Nam.

That way lies disaster.

Santayana once said that those who ignore history are doomed to repeat it. To learn from our past is the only responsible way to gird ourselves for the future, particularly when that past is the record of a monumental failure.

Those who most strongly endorse Mr. Ford's sentiment seem in the very next breath to be defying their own counsel by reasserting the old Westmoreland-Goldwater-Kissinger line: "If only we had bombed the hell out of them, the war would have been over years ago." How wistfully the President told General Westmoreland only a few weeks ago that he could not follow his advice to resume bombing Hanoi and mining Haiphong harbor, because "there's a law against that, Westy."

I do not want people who think that way to urge the rest of us "to put Viet Nam behind us." If we do, there will soon be another Viet Nam before us.

We have learned different things from Viet Nam, and we need to engage in enough public debate to sort out which are important to remember, and for what reasons. I hope that Gerald Ford, for example, will learn some of the things William Sloane Coffin learned; that our Congresspeople will remember what it cost the world when they were captured (or at least captivated) by the Pentagon mentality, particularly at budget time; that Walt Rostow will reassess the "light at the end of the tunnel" metaphor.

I hope that members of churches and synagogues will ask themselves why they were so reluctant to condemn the war; that Billy Graham will reflect on why an evangelist of the Prince of Peace never condemned the war at all. I hope the hawks will count the graves, and the doves will see if they can distinguish their position from isolationism.

I hope there are some things we can *all* learn and tell one another, so that we can never, never forget.

111

— Let us learn that this war could be waged only because our leaders lied to us. When the people of our country discovered what was really going on, their outrage finally overcame the lies, and the war ended. A left-handed tribute to human decency.

— Let us learn that the spirit of a people can be more powerful than a whole sky-full of B-52's, and that we could not bend a small nation to our will, even with the most merciless bombing in history.

ECOLOGICAL DESTRUCTION

Mr. President, suppose we took gigantic bull-dozers and scraped the land bare of trees and bushes at the rate of 1,000 acres a day or 44-million square feet a day until we had flattened an area the size of the State of Rhode Island, 750,000 acres.

Suppose we flew huge planes over the land and sprayed 100-million pounds of poisonous herbi-cides on the forests until we had destroyed an area of prime forests the size of Massachusetts or 5½ million acres.

Supppose we flew B-52 bombers over the land dropping 500-pound bombs until we had dropped almost 3 pounds per person for every man, woman, and child on earth — 8 billion pounds — and created 23 million craters on the land measuring 26 feet deep and 40 feet in diameter....

Suppose the land destruction involves 80 percent of the prime forests and 10 percent of all the cultivated land in the Nation.

We would consider such a result a monumental catastrophe. That is what we have done to our ally, South Vietnam.

Senator Gaylord Nelson quoted from the **Congressional Record** in the **Christian Science Monitor**, May 10, 1972.

— Let us learn that we were victims of the erosion of moral constraint, and that one day's unthinkable thought became the next day's do-able deed. We — not just "they" — shot civilians, tortured prisoners, bombed hospitals, napalmed children and gave medals to those who did so. A right-handed tribute to human depravity.

— Let us learn that we committed "war crimes." If the standards by which we executed Nazi leaders after World War II were applied to us (as we announced at Nuremberg they should be), what would this mean? Difficult as it is to contemplate, it would mean that not only should Lt. Calley have been convicted but also General Westmoreland, Lyndon Johnson, Richard Nixon, Dean Rusk, Henry Kissinger and many other major policymakers.

And by any moral reckoning the rest of us who consented to their deeds should be implicated in the legal reckoning against them. There will be no such convictions, but the recognition that there should have been might deter the repetition of such crimes by future policymakers. An evenhanded tribute to human justice.

— Let us learn that those who act as "policemen of the world" are not welcomed by those they choose to police. Our "enemies" resisted us, while our "friends" were either corrupted by us or corrupted us. The "bloodbaths" we sought to avert were miniscule compared to the bloodbaths (no quotation marks) we engineered.

— Let us learn that the right of dissent is both precious and fragile. The major spokespeople of both Democratic and Republican administrations equated dissent with disloyalty if not with treason. It was our youth who saved us. The simple (and costly) act of refusing to kill Vietnamese counted for more than administration rhetoric or threats. A clear argument for unconditional amnesty.

— Let us learn that we need not trust "experts." All their predictions were wrong, especially the Pentagon's annual prediction that a few more billion dollars and a few more thousand lives would bring the elusive "victory" within our grasp.

— Let us learn that most who protested the war did too little too late, that the nation's moral leaders spoke

113

with timid voices and muted deeds, and that we all pre-
ferred not to discern the signs of the times when they
threatened our personal security.

That will do for starters. What might we make of
such lessons?

First, we need to find sufficient grace to admit that
we were wrong: wrong to get in, wrong to stay in.
Nations do not make such concessions easily if at all.
But it might inaugurate a new era in international relations if we could do so. The rest of the world knows we
were wrong. Let us not become the only people who do
not know the truth about us. Let history at least record
that we were more honest in accepting defeat than in
pursuing victory.

Second, we need to make amends. How can we do
that? No one can raise up the dead. But someone might
raise up new homes, schools and hospitals. Someone
might reseed the bombed-out rice fields, replant the
defoliated forests.

Not us. At least not directly and certainly not ini-
tially, for what Indochinese Asians are going to want
many of us back to ''save'' their countries for a second
time? But having spent many billions for destruction,
we have an obligation to spend commensurate billions
for reconstruction. Food-and-goods-and-money-
through - international - agencies - with - no - strings-
attached constitutes the prescription that will enable
the Indochinese to make their own decisions about their
rebuilding.

Third, we need to grasp the hard truth that what we
did openly in Viet Nam is what we do furtively elsewhere: We attempt to impose our will on the people of
other nations. Only the means are different. In Chile we
used the CIA instead of napalm, dollars instead of
bombers, economic pressure instead of ground troops.
The scenario is similar, whether the place is Greece,
Spain, Brazil or the Philippines. The open scenario
failed in Viet Nam. The furtive scenario will not work
elsewhere.

Is it conceivable that we could move in new direc-
tions? It is conceivable. But not by forgetting Viet Nam.

Only by remembering it.

Otherwise we are surely doomed to repeat it.

Editorial cartoon by Wright in the **Miami Daily News**
Reprinted with permission

EXERCISE **6**

DISTINGUISHING PRIMARY FROM SECONDARY SOURCES

A critical thinker must always question his various sources of information. Historians, for example, usually distinguish between **primary sources** (eyewitness accounts) and **secondary sources** (writings based on primary or eyewitness accounts, or other secondary sources.) A diary written by a Civil War veteran is one example of a primary source. In order to be a critical reader one must be able to recognize primary sources. However, this is not enough. Eyewitness accounts do not always provide accurate descriptions. Historians may find ten different eyewitness accounts of an event and all the accounts might interpret the event differently. Then they must decide which of these accounts provide the most objective and accurate interpretations.

Test your skill in evaluating sources by participating in the following exercise. Pretend you are living 2000 years in the future. Your teacher tells you to write an essay about the causes of the growing American public opposition to U.S. military intervention in Indochina between 1965 and 1975. Consider carefully each of the following source descriptions. First, **underline** only those descriptions you feel would serve as a primary source for your essay. Second, **rank** only the underlined or primary sources assigning the number (1) to the most objective and accurate primary source, number (2) to the next most accurate and so on until the ranking is finished. Then discuss and compare your evaluations with other class members.

Assume that all of the following sources deal with the broad topic of the growing public opposition to our military intervention in Indochina.

_____ 1. A book in 1980 by former Senator J. William Fulbright, a prominent critic of U.S. military intervention in Indochina

_____ 2. A radio and television national address by Lyndon B. Johnson, given in 1964 while he was the President

_____ 3. A taped interview in 1974 of a member of the U.S. Army's Charlie Company that committed the Mylai massacre of Vietnamese women and children

_____ 4. A national address by Richard M. Nixon given while he was still the President in 1973

_____ 5. A book in 1970 by Bernard Fall, a well known American scholar of Vietnamese culture

_____ 6. A book in 1974 by a scholar of Vietnamese culture who is a citizen of India

_____ 7. An essay in 1975 by an American sociologist who specializes in the study of American social attitudes

_____ 8. A speech by Ho Chi Minh in 1967

_____ 9. A senate speech in 1982 by Senator John Tower of Texas, a prominent supporter of American military intervention in Indochina

SELECTED PERIODICAL BIBLIOGRAPHY

The editor has compiled a periodical bibliography. For the student's convenience, it is organized into three topical areas that relate to the three chapters in the text. It is hoped that the following titles will be helpful to students searching for more information about issues presented in this book.

THE WAR YEARS

Stephen E. Ambrose — *The Failure of a Policy Rooted in Fear*, **The Progressive**, November, 1970, pp. 14-20.

William F. Buckley, Jr. — *End of Vietnamization*, **National Review**, January 19, 1973, pp. 110-11.

James Burnum — *Is It All Over in Vietnam?* **National Review**, April 28, 1972, p. 449.

Commonweal — *Peace Now*, January 5, 1973, pp. 291-92.

Zalin B. Grant — *It's That Kind of War*, **The New Republic**, December 20, 1969, pp. 9-11.

Human Events — *Saigon Ambassador: Viet Aid Critical*, February 22, 1975, pp. 6, 15.

Erwin Knoll — *The Mysterious Project Phoenix*, **The Progressive**, February, 1970, pp. 19-22.

Thomas A. Lane — *The U.S. Must Prove Its Worth in South Vietnam*, **Human Events**, April 5, 1975, pp. 12-13.

David Lawrence — *How to End the War in Vietnam*, **U.S. News & World Report**, April 24, 1972, p. 104.

Gordon Livingston	*The Enemy Is Us*, **The Progressive**, November, 1970, pp. 32-34.
Eliot Marshall and Tom Geoghegan	*Calculating the Costs*, **The New Republic**, February 10, 1973, pp. 21-22.
Senator Gale W. McGee	*Vietnam: A Living Example for Implementing the American Spirit*, **Vital Speeches of the Day**, May 1, 1960, pp. 440-43.
W. S. Merrick	*Latest Report on a War with No Winner, No End*, **U.S. News & World Report**, September 25, 1972. pp. 40-42.
Nation	*Cost of Nixon's Peace Plan*, September 4, 1972, pp. 132-33.
National Review	*Bombing and Morality*, January 19, 1973, p. 74 + .
Newsweek	*Diplomacy by Terror; What the Bombing Did*, January 8, 1973, pp. 10-12.
Michael Novak	*Rights and Wrongs*, **The New Republic**, February 10, 1973, pp. 31-32.
Madson Pirie	*The Tiger Cages Revisited*, **National Review**, September 27, 1974, p. 103.
The Progressive	*The Terrible Realities; Letters from a GI in Vietnam*, January, 1970, pp. 14-18.
Senate Hearings	Hearings before the Senate Committee on Foreign Relations. These hearings beginning in the mid 1960's and continuing into 1975 present students with one of the best sources on American policy in Southeast Asia.
I. F. Stone	*McNamara and Tonkin Bay: The Unanswered Questions*, **The New York Review of Books**, March 28, 1968.
Time	*They Made a Revolution*, November 6, 1972, p. 30.

WHY OUR POLICY FAILED

Robert L. Bard — *The Mayaguez Mistake*, **The Christian Century**, June 4, 1975, pp. 564-65.

Anthony T. Bouscaren — *What Happened?* **National Review**, June 20, 1975, pp. 660-66.

Allan C. Brownfield — *Liberals to Blame for Cambodian Slaughter*, **Human Events**, August 9, 1975, p. 10.

William F. Buckley, Jr. — *On the Collapse of South Vietnam*, **National Review**, April 25, 1975, p. 470.

James Burnum — *It's All Your Fault*, **National Review**, April 25, 1975, p. 441.

Richard A. Falk — *Vietnam: The Final Deceptions*, **The Nation**, May 17, 1975, pp. 582-84.

Frances FitzGerald — *The End is the Beginning*, **The New Republic**, May 3, 1975, pp. 7-8.

David Halberstam — *Why It Never Worked*, **Newsweek**, April 14, 1975, p. 11.

Norman B. Hannah — *The Great Strategic Error*, **National Review**, June 20, 1975, pp. 666-69.

Jeffrey Hart — *Liberal Betrayal of Vietnam Shows Suicide Impulse*, **Human Events**, April 12, 1975, p. 8.

Senator Mark O. Hatfield — *Vietnam; A Sobering Postscript*, **Post American**, May 1975, pp. 6-7.

Stanley Hoffmann — *The Sulking Giant*, **The New Republic**, May 3, 1975, pp. 15-17.

Colonel Robert J. Heinl, Jr. — *A Critique of the Vietnam War*, **Human Events**, March 3, 1973, pp. 12, 14, 16.

George McT. Kahin — *The Secret War*, **The New Republic**, May 3, 1975, p. 13-14.

Stanley Karnow — *Grand Illusion*, **The New Republic**, May 3, 1975, pp. 8-10.

Anthony Lewis — *Hubris, National and Personal*, **The New Republic**, May 3, 1975, pp. 17-19.

John D. Lofton, Jr.	*Congress Guilty of Vietnam Sellout*, **Human Events**, April 12, 1975, p. 8.
National Review	*Looking Back on Vietnam*, April 25, 1975, p. 451 + .
Time	*How Should Americans Feel?* April 14, 1975, p. 27.
U.S. News & World Report	*End in Vietnam*, May 12, 1975, pp. 16-19.

LESSONS AND CONSEQUENCES

Atlas Report	*After Vietnam*, June, 1975, pp. 27-38.
William F. Buckley, Jr.	*On the Bloodbath*, **National Review**, May 23, 1975, pp. 576-77.
James Burnum	*Reflections on Defeat*, **National Review**, May 23, 1975, p. 549.
Edward L. Ericson	*America Enters a Post-Vietnam Era*, **The Humanist**, July, August, 1975, pp. 5-6.
M. Stanton Evans	*Agonizing Reappraisals in Southeast Asia*, **Human Events**, June 7, 1975, p. 7.
Howard Flieger	*Time to Look Forward*, **U.S. News & World Report**, April 28, 1975, p. 84.
Senator Barry Goldwater	*The Only Lesson to Be Learned from Vietnam War*, **Human Events**, July 5, 1975, p. 14.
Judith M. Hughes and Stuart Hughes	*Notes for a Foreign Policy*, **The Nation**, June 7, 1975, pp. 690-92.
Bill Moyers	*Last Reflections on a War*, **Newsweek**, April 21, 1975, p. 100.
National Review	*Showing a Little Class; Welcoming the Refugees*, May 23, 1975, p. 540.
National Review	*Our Vietcong, 'Tis of Thee*, June 20, 1975, p. 653.
The New Republic	*Learning the Wrong Lessons*, February 1, 1975, pp. 5-8.

The New Republic
On the Disasters of the Indochina War, May 3, 1975 (This entire issue is devoted to an analysis of the Indochina War).

Gareth Porter
Vietnam: Reconciliation Begins, **The Christian Century**, June 11-18, pp. 600-602.

The Executive Officers of the National Council of Churches
Cleanse Us of Arrogance, **The Christian Century**, May 7, 1975, p. 462.

U.S. News & World Report
Military Men Bitter After Vietnam? What a Survey Shows, June 16, 1975, pp. 45-46.

Jim Wallis
Vietnam and Repentance, **Post American**, May, 1975, pp. 17-21.

Charles A. Wells
Finale in S.E. Asia; Why No Victory? **Between the Lines**, April 15, 1975, pp. 1-2.

meet
the editors

Gary E. McCuen received his A.B. degree in history from Ripon College. He also has an M.S.T. degree in history from Wisconsin State University in Eau Claire, Wisconsin. He has taught social studies at the high school level and is currently working on additional volumes for the Opposing Viewpoints Series.

HIEBERT LIBRARY

3 6877 00113 5648

DAVID L. BENDER is a history graduate from the University of Minnesota. He also has an M.A. in government from St. Mary's University in San Antonio, Texas. He has taught social problems at the high school level and is currently working on additional volumes for the Opposing Viewpoints Series.